LIFE

DESCENT from and

ASCENT to

the AWARENESS of

WHO YOU REALLY ARE

John McIntosh

Published by Aurelio Enzo Productions Inc.

ISBN: 9781792977053

I gratefully acknowledge Solveig Larsen for providing the image for the cover and those that appear within this book

INDEX

PART ONE
THE DESCENT
The Downward Spiral

PART TWO
AWAKENING
The Doldrums

PART THREE
THE ASCENT
The Upward Spiral

DEDICATION

*You have never been, nor are you, nor will you
[ever] be estranged from Reality*

You are the fullness of Perfection here and Now

*Nothing can deprive you of your heritage of
What You Are*

-Nisargadatta

This book is dedicated to one who exemplifies this Truth. She has mingled at the summit of every glamor the grand dream has to offer, but the gentle and persistent tug of Un-Conditioned Love could not be ignored and from an early age her Life has extended this Love to the world.

The delicate fragrance of this beautiful Light touched my Heart and has drawn me deeper and deeper into IT. I am profoundly grateful for the privilege of Knowing her. *Her name is* Solveig, *which means path of the sun.*

INTRODUCTION

NOW is another name for
Pure Conscious Awareness ...
NOT a tiny fraction of time

Within the simple sketch of the *Descending* and *Ascending* spiral of Conscious Awareness outlined in this book, the *essence* is that

All is Well
Nothing is Broken and
Nothing is a Mistake

The universe and more particularly the planet and your own personal association with it, are NOT in jeopardy. Ideally, you will come away from this book at least with this:

-Nothing has ever been out of place

-YOU have never done anything wrong

-You are Perfect in every way

-Returning HOME is a certainty

-YOU are Loved UN-Conditionally always, no matter what.

You may also realize that:

-No matter where you find yourself consciously, you can return HOME in this lifetime. This means full Conscious Awareness that You Are the I AM Presence and have just forgotten this Truth

-This is far simpler than most belief systems suggest

It is important to understand that no matter how deep Consciousness **Descends** into the grand dream ... it will always **Ascend** back into full Awareness of Who IT Really IS. That relentlessness is in *full swing* throughout the planet Now and as a result is having a massive effect on humanity's return HOME.

This book will offer an overview of the *Descent* from full *Conscious Awareness of Who You Really Are* to *Awakening* when you realize on some level that you have been living within a dream. It will outline the pitfalls that can leave you lingering in this false-freedom zone for many lifetimes and then go on to paint a picture of the eventual *Ascent back to full Conscious Awareness or the Freedom that You Are.*

This will be outlined in *very simple* terms with no reference at all to ancient teachings or complicated formulas and disciplines. Freedom is easy, IT only requires a total commitment which I call the NO MATTER WHAT choice. If you can make this choice and stick with it, genuine Freedom in this lifetime *is* possible.

*Note: Throughout this book instead of using the term **soul**, I use **God-SELF** to indicate the individuated sleeping God you have been and **SELF** or **Real SELF** to point to the fully Conscious version. Both represent the God You Are. I also speak of the **false self** or **body-mind-identity** instead of the **ego**. Both soul and ego have many connotations, which can confuse, and this book is about the **simplicity** of God's [Our] Descent, Awakening and Ascent of Conscious Awareness. Some things will be repeated often for emphasis.*

Your attachment to the way you believe things should be is one of the greatest causes of your suffering

PART ONE

THE DESCENT

The Downward Spiral

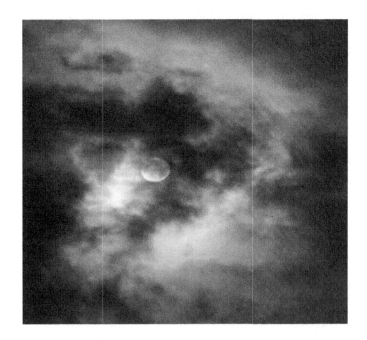

Chapter One

THE DESCENT OF AWARENESS OF WHO YOU REALLY ARE

LIFE is another word for Pure Conscious Awareness. It is also known as I AM, the SELF, God, Light, ONE and many other often more obscure names. It is *Who* You Really Are but is usually spoken of as a *separate* entity or experience.

"How is Life treating you? or
"Life is really tough, isn't it?"

Examples such as these illustrate how the *mind* places Life *outside* somewhere. ONE is always ONE, not ONE [Life] plus you. Nevertheless, if you believe you are a separate individual in a world of separated things and circumstances, Life *will* seem like something you *have* rather than something you *are*. There is a *vast* difference.

It is this separated sense of *being* that is the root of all suffering and *seems* to exist on a very wide scale between victim-hood and happiness.

The Un-Knowable Nothing-ness *IS* before ALL that *seems* to be. In order for the Un-Knowable to taste experience … to *know* IT SELF, IT uses *Consciousness* as a body. ALL THAT IS, *is* Consciousness *appearing* as very solid holographic projections, which are a play of Light appearing as *matter* and *experience*. The entire universe and everything in it including your body and everything that seems to be happening *is* this projection.

It is *all* temporary, coming and going with a beginning and an ending. As such it is NOT Real. This is why it is often referred to as an illusion or a dream. Consciousness steps into ALL these projections and experiences them *as* Life and plays *with* them to *know* IT SELF.

THE UNKNOWABLE
[Who You Really Are]
[uses]
Consciousness-God-I AM-Light-Life-ONE
[as ITs body]

DESCENT
Attention on Experiences

Projected Stories & Dramas

Separation/Sleep To Who You Really Are

Frustration/Satiation

Attention on Freedom

AWAKENING
[Leading to Self Discovery]

ASCENT

*Pure Conscious Awareness of
Who You Really Are as*

THE UNKNOWABLE

Everything has this ONE Life within it *at various levels* of Conscious Awareness of IT SELF, as the God IT *is*. At the level of a human, a dream within a dream occurs, which most know as *free will*. There is only one Will and that is the Will of the *God* You Are. While human Consciousness sleeps within the dream of separation it believes it has a *separate free will*.

This dream of *free will* expands the sense of separation. Before this dream of a separated *will*, Life [Consciousness] knows it exists as ONE. The mother bear or wolf sees its offspring as an extension of itself. A tree communicates with *all* trees in existence. The Earth is ONE entity. The grain of sand on the beach is aware of itself as the mountain on the other side of the world. ALL Life is ONE. The human Consciousness however, believes it is alone, as a separated entity, and here is where *suffering* arises from the belief in the possibility of *victims*.

Victim-hood *seems* to exist when comparisons are made between have's and have-nots in a multitude of situations. This allows the concept of suffering to exist *before* anything occurs, disguised as a *future possibility* that might occur and thereby causes another layer of suffering.

The belief in separation, comparison, victim-hood and suffering gives rise to all manner of *conditioning* which is made up of all *attachments, expectations* and *identifications* tied to *memory*. And Life, which has NO identity whatsoever, then assumes a myriad of roles making up a *false identity* in each human form.

This is the *descended* version of Consciousness which has taken on the *dream* role as a *false self,* which can also be called the body-mind-identity or who most people call *myself.* This is a mercurial identity which is constantly changing as more and more conditioning is added.

For example, in the false self's opinion [the Real SELF has no opinions … IT simply *Knows*], there is a thing called *self-esteem.* This is the measuring rod that identifies one's level of *worth* in what it believes is a competitive world, again which comes about as a result of its belief in separation.

Many organizations and services exist around the world to enhance this *made-up belief* in self-esteem. The entire *self -improvement* industry is based on the belief that the false self can be improved but what is an illusion cannot be affected in any way that is Real and the True SELF is already Perfect and can not be changed in any way at all.

You, the Real YOU, *is* Pure, Perfect, Complete – ONE.

The false self makes you feel small, limited and of little significance during the gradually Descending spiral of Conscious Awareness.

At the same moment it will tell you that it is leading you HOME, that you are better than you believe and that things are getting better.

In this way it is taking with one hand and giving with the other trying to convince you that 'it' is who you are. This tactic has been very effective for countless eons and most of humanity still lingers in the illusion of this individual person-hood where fear is its constant companion.

Chapter Two

THE FALSE 'I'

The life the *false 'I' ...* the false self experiences, carries a heavy weight. It wears *many masks*, literally living several different lives and these require vast amounts of mind-thought to *bring-off* these deceptions, *especially from itself.* The more invested one is in professing the validity of who they are currently portraying themselves to be, the more mind-knowledge must be carried and applied at just the right moments.

Its like an actor who plays multiple characters in a movie like the quick-artistry of Robin Williams in Mrs. Doubtfire, which eventually became so complicated it was exposed as fake. Most of the roles the false self plays are unconscious shifts, which adapt from moment to moment. The superficial hellos and greetings, the obsequious fawning to those who may offer something of value, the flowers and chocolates given from a sense of obligation, the presents exchanged as repayment for receiving the same, the clothing worn to please others but secretly hated.

Authentic living is not known to the false self even when it says *enough* and puts its foot down in angry frustration as the pendulum of behavior swings to the opposite extreme toward defiance … neither is real.

The Real You, the fully Conscious God-SELF *Lives Life Lightly*. It has no *attachments* to what the world thinks and lives in the moment spontaneously. It has no *expectations* of HOW Life should play out, saying YES always to *What Is*. This means that IT does not resist *What Is* and as a result does not carry the weight of the anger and judgment that comes with resistance. That does NOT mean that IT agrees with what is.

IT knows that *resistance* has the same effect as *support* because it is a form of *focused Attention*, which is the conduit for the *Life-Force* that keeps manifested things and experiences *alive* and *expands* them. The concept of *forgiveness* is this non-resistant Awareness. Forgiveness is *always for* the God-SELF and never for the false-self-identity.

When the God-SELF is fully Conscious IT *identifies* IT SELF with nothing. If IT happens to be acting as a doctor or a pilot or an artist for example, IT will *NOT* refer to IT SELF as these identities. IT knows they are temporary costumes and if anything, IT will simply say IT is temporarily doing or acting the part of these made up identities.

IT never confines IT SELF to less than the *infinite* All That Is. The God-SELF Truly *is nothing* as well as *All That Is* ... a Divine Dichotomy *Living Life Lightly.*

Ever Shifting Landscape

No so-called positive *change* that occurs within the ever-shifting landscape of events in the grand dream humanity calls life *has any effect whatsoever* on the *conditioning* that brought them about. For example, if all child abuse on the planet were to end today through some massive global effort, the unique blend of conditioning in the collective false self that manifested these circumstances would find another outlet, perhaps totally disguised and seemingly unrelated.

On a personal level when for example *unworthiness* manifests in a relationship through one partner, abuse of various kinds may show up from a dominating spouse who belittles and constantly puts their partner down, to full scale physical violence. This *blatant mirror* will be repeated, perhaps through similar partnerships on an endless loop of circumstances that seem to validate the belief in the *lack of worthiness.*

Or, perhaps the abuses have reached a point where such experiences will no longer be tolerated and instead of *turning within* toward the real cause, that one chooses to live alone. In such cases *anger, hatred* and *rage* may fan the flames of the conditioning expanding its insidious influence ... often well beneath the surface where it can simmer in a stew of bitterness further entrenching the original conditioning. The conditioning however, when it has shown up in one's face *will* find another way to express itself.

In such a case the slights, condemnations and generic abuses will find other mirrors that trigger this one's conditioning such as in the work environment or through social activities. It is also common for instance, for one who has chosen to turn their back on the *outward* and *personal* perpetrators, to support *causes* that attempt to fight and eliminate such manifestations. Then, the very *Attention* paid to the subject provides a conduit for the *Life-Force* that flows through attention to *expand* the existence of the conditioning and its manifested forms.

This is why *fighting for peace* actually *expands conflict*. So deep is the sleep of the collective false self that this very obvious outcome has been completely missed by countless millions throughout the ages.

Finally, when the sleeping God-SELF has been sufficiently triggered that it *begins* to *turn inward* for answers, often the false self will shift gears and seek to circumvent any real Awareness by directing life experiences [in this example] toward *mind solutions* such as self-improvement, defense training, assertiveness teachings and a very wide variety of ways and means to shore up the illusionary concept of *self-esteem* so that it can better navigate the shark infested waters the false self believes exists everywhere.

These kinds of band-aid approaches are very popular ways of attempting to *handle* and *control* one's life and often bear sufficient *initial fruit* to keep one immersed in these fantasies for lifetimes through new combinations of conditioning.

Eventually, the God-SELF becomes satiated enough that IT recognizes these techniques never really change life for the so called better ... either on a personal level or macrocosmically on a global scale. The mirrors are often harsh and the suffering long but ultimately the blessing in them is seen through an ocean of tears and the sleeping God-SELF unswervingly *turns completely inward* toward IT SELF.

Karma

The concept of karma [also known as cause and *inevitable* effect] has a very large following but what is tied to time and space is NOT real. It exists only *within the dream* as a persistent influence and when one steps into the NOW where time and space have no existence, new karma cannot be created.

There *is* however a residual influence or momentum like an automobile that has been travelling at a certain speed that is suddenly turned off. The forward movement will continue until inertia brings it to a halt. When Consciousness is Aware of IT SELF as the God-SELF or Life that IT is, if it remains in a physical body it will, for a while continue to experience this momentum but IT is *now "Living IN the dream [world] not OF it"* and the suffering associated with the belief in separation and victims has dissolved so that the momentum ceases to molest ITs experiences.

Reincarnation

Reincarnation is also time-bound and as such is NOT real. It is a dream within the grand dream. Whatever has a beginning [a lifetime] and an ending, no matter how often it seems to take place for the sleeping God-SELF, *exists only as a dream experience.* Whatever conditioning [which defines who you believe yourself to be] that has *not* been transformed at the end of one dream life will have as many dream life opportunities to be transformed as are required.

Chapter Three

ATTENTION

Attention is what most would call the instrument of creating. When used for its *True Purpose* it is the magic wand of Freedom. It is the conduit through which Life-Force flows bringing forth manifested things and experiences *and* Shifts.

In the world of dreams when *Attention* is combined with *Passion* and *Activity*, whatever that attention has been placed on *will* come forth … *if not tampered with.*

Dream/Idea + Attention + Passion + Activity

= Manifestation

It is one's conditioning that tampers with the manifestation, which brings about a still-born dream/idea or a manifested *tainted* version of it colored by a *combination of conditioning* that redesigns what was intended.

For example, if one is attached to being *recognized*, the dreamer's essence will appear everywhere within the manifestation … perhaps a building or a company, as an expression of grandeur. The images the collective consciousness has of the originating dreamer will radiate throughout the structure touching and influencing everything associated with it.

This may at first seem an ideal situation particularly since the false self applauds certain visible examples of what it calls success, but always these are the chains [in this case *attachment*] that bind the God-SELF to limitation no matter how grand the manifested results may appear.

It is the neutral and simple manifestations that serve as a pure conduit through which the fully Conscious God-SELF may flow in all its Beauty and Abundance.

Symbols have the same influence. For example, for many thousands of years the meaning of the swastika was *well-being* to a wide variety of religious orders and countries. It is only since the 2nd World War that it has carried an ominous distinction. This is a clear indication of how conditioning effects manifestation, in this case the manifestation of a global perspective.

Even when one's dream *does* manifest it will usually fail to bring about the resulting feelings the designer intended due to their conditioning.

Most of humanity and its endless made up world is experiencing wide spread expansion of these frustrating results at this very moment.

For example, if one has a dream of great wealth, power, influence and fame as a means to enjoy a happy life and, if the conditioning of *unworthiness* [in some way] is present, as it is with most people to some degree, the result will lack the desired outcome with the exception of surface appearances. This was the key element that forced me off the cliff of dreams in 1999.

The sense of being invisible or NOT seen was the primary conditioning *I picked up* as a child and was an aspect of the root conditioning of unworthiness that I *re-acquired* from past lifetimes in this lifetime in order to *transform* it. There *are no mistakes nor blame* in who we choose as our parents or guardians, it's all part of the return HOME.

This principal influence touched everything in my life from then on, and although I *did* manifest every dream I ever had as a false self, the happiness and fulfilment I expected to accompany it was never present. I was a multi-millionaire but lived like a pauper within.

A similar *end result* of all manifested things and experiences always occurs when the false self is the designer of your life because the false-self - identity, which is defined by its conditioning [attachments, expectations, identifications and the memories associated with them] taints all of them.

It is a closed loop of repeated results until the frustration inherent in these results brings one to their knees where they begin to look for a deeper understanding of how Life *really* functions. In this regard Life has *used dysfunction* to bring one to Truth, which is an enormous blessing. Everything in life *bends* toward your Freedom in some way.

If you believe anything with enough *passion* and the appropriate *activity* [if required], it *will become* your dream-experience *NOT your reality* … that too is a dream. There *is* only one exception and that is the Attention on the Pure Conscious Awareness that You Are.

Road Blocks

On the *Descent* of Consciousness and well into the *Ascent* the false self sets up road blocks everywhere to make Freedom *seem* difficult and thereby delay the end of its reign of tyranny when the Freedom You Are returns to your Conscious Awareness. This return *is* simple …

difficult but *simple*. When Attention is *withdrawn* from anything the Life Force flowing through Attention is also withdrawn and the manifested [or manifesting] *Intention* upon which *Attention* was placed, fades back into nothing-ness.

Like a laptop whose power cord has been pulled out of the electrical socket, the reserve battery provides a certain momentum to continue for a short period but eventually it shuts down ... provided [Attention] the power cord connection, is not plugged in again.

However, the wispy *Intentions,* so common during the course of a day, which come and go in an instant, turn a trickling stream into a raging torrent when *consistent Attention* is combined with *Passion* and *Activity.* If your Attention is caught up in one [likely several] of the false self's traps, the road blocks *you yourself are giving Life to,* can remain for the rest of your life thereby distracting you from Real Freedom.

There are many *sacred-cows* in humanity's dream experience, which the false self uses to create road blocks such as special dates on the calendar, figures in authority, heroes and heroines from a wide variety of conflicts, the concept of justice, borders between countries, ideas surrounding righteousness, global causes and a host of others. Whether *respected* or *resented* a certain *devotion* or *resistance* is experienced with regard to these made-up entities and that constitutes *Attention*, which can be *very powerful* depending on how intense your *focus* is on the subject.

The same thing spills over into each individual's life with regard to their unique circumstances. The life experience of the dreamer is one of walking on egg shells or trampling on them depending one one's level of frustration with *what is, what they feel it should be* or *what seems to be*. It's a chess board of constantly moving pieces with limitless possibilities that control the *Intentions* behind thoughts, words and deeds from moment to moment ... most of it below the level of Conscious Awareness.

In some way, virtually anything that is NOT directly focused on the return HOME to the LIFE You Really Are ... *is* a distraction and therefore a road block.

Chapter Four

SYMPTOMS OF THE DESCENT OF CONSCIOUSNESS

Stories

Once Consciousness has fully *Descended* and immersed IT SELF in the dream of separation with layer upon layer of conditioning coiled around IT making up the false-self-identity, IT refers to this entity as *'me or myself'*. IT has then become fully *distracted* from ITs True Identity as Life or God.

There IT remains for eons wrapped up in the grand dream exchanging role after role as IT plays every conceivable character from arch villain to sublime saint. No story is greater than the dramas told by the *victim* who often masquerades as a severely wounded *hero,* the martyr of great sacrifice who has fallen on their sword for the benefit of all that is True ... that is, their version of Truth within a deluded cloud of conditioning.

The wider the swing of the pendulum from *grief* and *agony* to *grandiosity* and *happiness* is, as it seems to overcome the evils of the world, the more distractive the story is from the Awareness of Who They Really Are.

Songs and sonnets, books and soap operas are filled with these sagas which portray the great challenge of living in an unforgiving world filled with dark specters hiding around every corner. They speak of comrades in arms who understand and share your plight, offering you a release valve to blow off the enormous build up of pressure just to get through a single day.

This repeating loop lasts for many lifetimes as Consciousness clings tightly to the victim's costume.

The illusion of limitation is greatest as the hapless, hopeless victim but the sense of *unworthiness* [the deepest conditioning of all] is a close imitator of nothing-ness, which lies at the *core* of Who You Really Are.

It is another Divine Dichotomy that at the furthest arc *away from Truth*, Consciousness is so *close to it*. Always, the long journey *out there* is about Awareness and never about distance, the sibling of time and the original sculptor of the belief in separation.

It *is* possible in an instant for the one caught in the *littleness-limitation-illusion* to have a *Grand Awakening* to Who They Really Are. You are never more than a glimpse away from total and complete Awareness of the God – the Life You Are.

Dramas

Imagine a stadium filled with tens of thousands of cheering and adoring fans applauding you for some special ability, talent or gift you are sharing with them. This is the usually *unconscious* but pervasive longing of every false self who is desperate for the validating response of the dream it calls reality.

This is what makes the roller coaster of happiness and sorrow *endurable* for the false self and offers the *juice*, the sense of *being alive* within the illusion that represents life in the body-mind-identity. Enormous sacrifices [in its eyes] are made in order to bring about, on some level, the constant need for a *fix* that confirms that it is in some way *real* proving it does indeed *exist.*

The underlying and haunting sense of life being a *sham* is present in all sleepers. This incessant *dripping-water-torture* is a gift from the Real SELF as IT ceaselessly reminds the imitator of Life that it is NOT real. In this way IT is constantly encouraging the sleeping God-SELF to come HOME.

It is a frequent specter in the life of entertainment heroes for example, that they feel [and are often told] that they are no better than their last achievement and that they must always be on guard lest they forfeit their moment in the sun. The distractive sedations available to squash this deep angst are often used by these icons who exemplify the global conscious *neediness* of all deep sleepers to *feel* alive and, which end up bringing on the exact opposite feeling.

On some level ALL false selves are constantly creating story/dramas in order to experience *life-confirming* responses and today with the advent of global social networks a moment to moment opportunity exists to experience these mini-validations. This phenomena blatantly illustrates how great the *void* of worthiness is within the collective false self but it is also a giant mirror that presents the opportunity for this *conditioning* to be exposed and *transformed* thinning the veils that hide the Truth from the sleeping God-SELF.

While the false self looks for every opportunity to exercise its *mind tricks* to keep the sleeping God-SELF imprisoned, the Real SELF, the fully Conscious aspect of the God-SELF is always nudging IT SELF Awake.

The Many Masks of The Grand Dream

Like a string of seductive pearls the false self projects an endless thread of dream thoughts producing more and more *dysfunctional programs* emanating from the belief in separation. The false self covets the usurped throne it has stolen from the sleeping God-SELF and defends it *subtly* and *insidiously* while IT remains unaware of its false identity and later viciously when you, as the *Awakening* God-SELF become suspicious that is it is really NOT who you are.

Despite your long and deep sleep as the God-SELF You Are, you have longed to escape its manipulative clutches for lifetimes, but *the body-mind-false-self-identity* possesses many tricks and seductions to lure you back into its tangled web and for eons you have succumbed to its alluring diversions.

The primary root of this conditioning is *shame, guilt* and *remorse* with the core, as stated earlier, being *unworthiness*. This root system in turn expands into a system of branches that cover every conceivable delusion the false self can experience, again in your own distinctive way, which is why your world is uniquely your own [one planet and almost 8 billion worlds].

In The Beginning

When we, as the ONE God we Are, chose to create the universe as a playground in which we could experience [Know] OUR SELF, we elected to begin this grand adventure *unconscious* of Who We Really Are. This is like going to a movie before reading the book. The ancient scriptures refer to this as the Fall of Man [the Garden of Eden allegory] … known by similar stories elsewhere. In Truth it is the *Fall of Consciousness beneath the Awareness of Who IT Really IS.*

Pure Conscious Awareness [God – ONE - YOU] created the grand dream of the universe through the *illusion of separation* containing a myriad of opposites [male-female, light-dark, day-night, etc.], which allowed time and space to seem real. These are prerequisites for all *manifestation* to appear because for anything to *appear* and *seem separate* it must be *apart* from something else taking time to *navigate* from and to.

IT/WE then stepped into every bit of the grand dream *as* LIFE from the so-called tiniest particle to the most massive manifestations, *everything* is ALIVE with/as our God-Consciousness at various levels of Awareness. The body-mind-identity or human is a *self-aware* manifestation and for eons has referred to itself as an *individual* thereby *seeming* to validate the reality of separation.

It is *in* this human form that God-Consciousness has the potential to re-awaken to Who IT Really Is and as another Divine Dichotomy it is the *dysfunctional programming* itself that allows this to occur.

This dysfunctional programming began when the God You Are seemed to *banish* IT SELF from the Garden of ONE-ness. The separated consciousness that seemed to exist in the manifested grand dream within the individual had the *sense* that it had been *abandoned* and this led to the feeling of *unworthiness*. It also led to *anger, rage* and *hatred* toward the God Consciousness, which then appeared to be a *separate, superior* and *judging* entity outside itself. This then led to the feelings of *remorse, guilt* and *shame* and the die was caste for the host of programs that make up the *conditioned false-self-identity*.

Some of the most influential programs that foster the dysfunctional life experiences of the false self include, ***power, fame, wealth*** and ***sex***. These have constituted the high profile and seductive fly-paper that provided a *temporary fix* for the false self, helping to dilute the *molesting* influence of the conditioned identity you have called *myself.* But like all fixes, they expanded the impaired life of the false self, *descending* it deeper and deeper into the grand dream.

The false-self weaves these powerful weapons into the fabric of fascinating and interlocking stories and dramas that grasp your attention like the breaking news headlines of the tabloids that catch your eye while you are in the check-out line at the local grocery store.

Power

The belief in separation brings with it all manner of *dream-symptoms* with victim-hood standing out prominently. The false-self-body-mind-identity either *resists* this feeling or *embraces* it, which means it either *attacks* it or *worships* it as we see everywhere depending on how much power that individual mind *believes* it has.

If, as the person-hood experience expands, the sense of power becomes strong enough, the false-self will attempt to *attack* by exercising *control* in a wide variety of ways ranging from *subtle* and *covert* such as through the spoken and written word in advertising and propaganda or blatantly and obviously perhaps as a dictator of a country or simply as a domineering figure in one's own family setting.

In this way a degree of *artificial security* muffles the underlying terror that at any moment their house-of-cards life experience can come tumbling down. Fully Aware, the God-SELF knows *that there is no such thing as control* in a dream any more than grasping a handful of air in your fist is possible but this dream within a dream fantasy is very common for the false-self-body-mind-identity.

If the person-hood experience feels weak and vulnerable an attitude of obsequious behavior may develop in some way. The false-self could take on the role of a servant in some manner that may range from the obvious position itself such as a waiter or a maintenance person or they may take on a role as a public servant ranging all the way up to the leader of a country or company. Of course, there are many instances of people feeling *a deep sense of purpose* and *fulfilment* in these kinds of roles ... there is no blanket definition and certainly judgment is not a factor. Servitude, as an extension of one's conditioning can exist in the loftiest positions possible within the grand dream.

The God-SELF has *no hierarchy* since IT is ONE, but the false self agonizes within a maze of perceived levels that align with its unique conditioning.

If a role emanates from the use of *power* to mask the fear oriented to victim-hood, whatever role the false self takes on will be *inauthentic* and self-serving no matter how clever the mask may be.

Fame

Recognition, whether grand or microscopic helps to smother the feeling of *insignificance* often emanating from experiences of being unseen, passed over or put down. This form of conditioning can have the *appearance* of great achievement to other false selves [in truth … there *are* no others].

The false self who rises to prominence anywhere in the world resonates with the longing to BE somebody in a world where invisibility is so common. The fashion and cosmetic industries as well as the various entertainment industries have become god-makers particularly in the last hundred years. While priests and royalty were once the recipients of great fame and adoration, now high-profile models and headlining actors and musicians have become world renown with countless numbers of *'other'* false selves hanging upon their every word as well as their private lives.

The influence of *vicarious identification* often totally supersedes the obvious superficiality of the current heroes of world importance.

On a more common theme and far more frequently present within this *shame-oriented* conditioning, parents will often ride on the coat-tails of their children's local fame in sports and scholastic achievements.

Wealth

Material wealth in the form of money and possessions is the most overt display of conditioning in the false self's made-up identity. All fundamental conditioning [guilt, shame, remorse and unworthiness] influences the grasping need for wealth beyond what is required to provide for the basics needs of caring for the body. Everything Consciousness needs while it occupies the body will be provided for when one is Aware of Who They Really Are. *"In the hour of your need, it is given to you"* [paraphrasing], was the simple and powerful wisdom offered by a beautiful SELF-Aware individual long ago.

If one *who is* SELF-Aware, has a need for wealth *at any level* for their Life Purpose, it will most certainly become available to them without great effort as an aspect of what is Joy-filled to Consciousness. However, to the false-self-identity, enormous effort is usually exerted to bring about a status of wealth together with all manner of compromising behavior. In fact, it believes that this is a prerequisite for this false crown of achievement providing additional credibility to its made-up identity.

There is nothing inherently wrong with wealth, power or fame since everything is initially neutral within the grand dream. It is the *attachment* to it that triggers the *suffering* associated with it.

Sex

Sex is perhaps the most over-powering *energy fix* used by the false self to band-aid the suffering linked to the heavy load of conditioning that defines it. While Consciousness is conditioned the possibility of *unconditional Love* is *impossible* despite the frequent use of this term ... especially by spiritually oriented people.

Obviously, *any* conditioning colors and taints what the false self claims is *unconditional* or *real Love*. Simply claiming that the Love expressed is real does NOT make it so and the many layers of conditioning present in most false selves are so well hidden that they often genuinely believe their expressions of Love *are* real ... but, that is not possible. One must first be totally authentic *with themselves* before there is *any possibility* of *unconditioned Love.*

Rarely is this more present than in the act of sex where conditioning often comes out of hiding. Manipulation and control, whether aggressive or subtly passive, oozes from this most potent instrument of the false-self-identity. It may be known to the abuser or not but it is usually present at some level by both partners no matter how affectionate the relationship may seem.

Relationships [which always suggest and seem to validate the belief in separation], are the greatest *mirrors* for recognizing one's own conditioning being reflected back at them ... up close and personal on a daily basis. Never is this more prevalent than in the act of sex, which tends to mask the odor of conditioning for some time due to its passionate nature. Eventually however, what disgusts one the most *about their own conditioning* over-rides the heated exchanges of sex and as a natural extension ... conflict ensues.

Until one *turns inward* and recognizes the *giant gift* that the mirror of their world offers them to transform their own conditioning ... particularly close relationships, these conflicts, borne of looking *out there* and finger pointing, will continue to cause great suffering.

There are many other expressions that also represent powerful programs within the false self's conditioning. Here are a few of those that frequently appear in the *Descent* of Consciousness.

Emotions and Suffering

Emotions are an emanation of the mind-body-identity-false-self. They are *channels* through which conditioning can be expressed in the dream the false self lives within. They are *never* a true representation of Who You Really Are.

The *mental* and *emotional suffering* the false self endures is a direct manifestation of the belief in *victims* borne of the belief in *separation*. There is no such thing as a *victim*. The emotions flood through victim-hood Consciousness, expanding the experience of suffering and validating victim-hood to the false self through its agonizing masks.

The false self will respond to the statement that there are no victims as an *outrage* ... a monstrous lie devoid of all compassion, and it has many supporters. It will shout, *"You have no idea what I have suffered through for years."*

The ONE God You Are - appears as many and yet IT is NOT separated. You and all that suffer *are* God in disguise playing a vital role in the transformation of Consciousness back to the Awareness of IT SELF *as* God. Consider how suffering in one expression or many *opens* even the coldest, shut heart ... if only a little. This is God unveiling IT SELF *to* IT SELF.

Emotions and suffering *expand* the false self's dream of separation. Emotional needs are therefore signs of the belief in victims ... *the Real SELF has no needs of any kind.*

Depression

Depression is a very common experience expressed through the emotions. It is a gaping hollow pit of hopelessness that often has no obvious relationship to a story/drama the false self has been engaged in and for some can be a frequent experience.

Other times it can be tied directly to one or more unfulfilled life events where you feel helpless to alter the story in your favor. It can be related to chronic issues that seem to have no solutions and lead to persistent thoughts of simple escape all the way up to suicide.

It can feel like an *end of the line* scenario where you just cannot take it any longer and can seem like the darkest thing you have ever felt. All extreme *triggers*, especially persistent ones, *point* to conditioning that has fully gestated like a pregnancy ready to be birthed, and that has contributed to the God-SELF's long and deep sleep of separation and limitation.

Depression is often one of the most persistent aspects of conditioning and when it is NOT obviously related to a story/drama it is like an umbrella that hides *many* aspects of your conditioned false-self-identity that are *ready to be transformed.* Depression is often called *a cry for love* and in this case is a very accurate description because all *triggers* that offer you an unmistakable opportunity to dive beneath the story/drama and into the intangible feelings related to conditioning, are a giant *cry* to return to the *Love* You Are.

As a result, they are a power-filled urge to remember Who You Really Are. Self Discovery means *standing in the fire of who you are NOT* so that the veils that hide the Truth can be exposed and transformed. Depression could be called a *powerful inducement* toward this pathless-path to genuine Freedom. Let this be an *encouragement* that this depression/fire is really oriented to bringing you HOME to the Awareness of the God You Are and *not* some pathetic deficiency in yourself [the false self] that you must endure.

Self-Hatred

There is a simmering self-hatred within every false-self-identity and depending on what belief systems they may adhere to if any, this powerful influence may be promoted as a justifiable feeling through made-up concepts such as *original sin*. Similar *tricks of mind* appear in most belief systems in some form allowing those in authority to more easily control their followers.

Whether or not you are influenced by these fantasies, there is usually sufficient evidence in the archives of the false-self-identity to justify its self -loathing ... or so it believes. As long as the conditioning that defines the false self exists, there will be an endless supply of reasons to feel *less-than, unworthy* and *non-deserving.*

As indicated above *guilt, shame, remorse* and *unworthiness* constitute the root system of every false-self-identity influencing every thought, word and deed especially the concept of *deserving* or *NOT deserving*, which touches virtually every life experience ... usually without Conscious Awareness.

Slogans in advertising cater to this gremlin. *"You deserve ..."* is the tag-line tied to the promotion of a multitude of products and services and can be a highly seductive influence on behavior, especially when you are certain that you do NOT deserve ... so powerful is the suggestion that you might be *approved of* in some way.

In matters concerning the body's appearance, feelings of self hatred can run extremely high. This focus has fostered giant industries such as weight loss, fashion, cosmetics and plastic surgery. Since the false self always lives *out there* any feedback that suggests that it is accepted, approved of or ideally – *Loved*, is highly sought after with no sacrifice too high to pay. As such the false self is always trying to catch up to the *ideal image* of what it currently believes will bring it the most acceptance and therefore the happiest life.

Charity, at any level for example is often *a front* for the approval so critically needed and is often witnessed through highly visible philanthropic activities where a person or family-name figures prominently in the *good* works. Even the most devout charitable offerings are often underpinned by an insidious longing to be loved and appreciated, well beneath the radar of the false self's awareness. *Obviously, there are significant exceptions.*

When one reaches the line in the sand where Freedom becomes their number one priority, they must become a *ruthlessly authentic witness* to every mirror that points to these hidden personal agendas and resolve to *stand in the fire of who they are NOT* – NO MATTER WHAT until the Awareness of the absolute Freedom They Are has returned.

Being Unseen

To expand upon this powerful theme, nothing is more terrifying to the body-mind-false-identity than *not being seen. Scorn, shame, rebuke* and *outright condemnation* is vastly preferable to *being invisible.* The child who is ignored is the child whose innate feelings of unworthiness [all who are not yet FREE have this inbred feeling to some extent] will go on to define its life experience in dramatic ways as it grows older, whether overtly or subtly.

Acting out for me was how I manifested the agony of being unseen. Whether it was being a rebel every chance I got or being sullen and moody, I would do anything to feel I *existed.* Others may become tyrants, or power brokers on many playing fields, many will go into selling or acting where their voice and body language has the opportunity of creating a stage anywhere an audience of one or more might exist.

This is not a judgment of parents or institutions who are dismissive of children for whatever reason ... that is the *story.* It is the recognition of how the world is a *giant mirror* for the most significant veil hiding the God-SELF We Are, which is *unworthiness.* As always, these reflections can be and are *triggers* to take us deep inside, beneath the story-drama to the bedrock of all the conditioning that manifests the sleeping God-SELF who masquerades as an individual ... somehow outside ONE-ness.

This dark and terrible baggage that seems to plague so many is actually *an Angel at the gate* to Freedom shining Light on who you are NOT. As you will see in *Part Three – The Ascent,* when you give your undivided Attention to what this Light is showing you, the gate will soon dissolve along with the false self you have been carrying for eons like a bag of rocks on your back.

Education

The body-mind-identity loves education. It craves facts and accumulated knowledge, the more the better. It does NOT have access to the infinite *Knowing* the Real SELF does despite that infinite knowledge being immediately and always available.

"Knowledge is Power" is a well-known adage but when that knowledge is based on accumulated, memorized information which usually requires the addition of analysis, comparisons, fine tuning and a host of devices the false self uses from its ancient archives to decipher, translate and transmit it to other false selves … it is like trying to empty the ocean with a teaspoon.

Despite this *exhausting* process the *existing* educational system is *highly revered* and touted as a prerequisite for a so-called *successful* life. There are a few exceptions that medical science and the educational system cannot explain. For example, an *autistic savant*, which refers to individuals with autism who have extraordinary skills not exhibited by most people. The savant, labeled as *disabled*, seems to *know things* without the need for years of study and counseling.

In Truth, these beings have access to *infinite knowledge* much like the fully Conscious God-SELF who is empty and available. When one is Aware of Who They Really Are this knowledge is always accessible precisely when it is required and with no need whatsoever to store details as the mind does. *"In the hour of your need it is given to you"* is the way-less-way of the individuated fully Conscious God-SELF who is given what it requires *when* it is required and without effort.

Infinite Knowledge requires total *Trust*, which the false self does not possess since it lives in a world it totally *dis-trusts* and believes is dangerous, complicated and mysterious.

The basic understanding of language and numbers is all that one requires to *initially* navigate its physical experience. After that what is perfect for that life will *just show up* when it's required no matter how intricate it may seem, provided that one remains *open* and *available*. As humanity makes the shift from **mind-thought** to **heart-feelings** the educational system will change as it makes available this kind of effortless living.

"Until you know Who you Are, all your knowledge is only learned ignorance."
— Ramana

Formulas

The mind feels a sense of safety and security in formulas. A simple recipe, followed exactly, will render the same cake, stew or soup every time. Consistency in results allows the false self to rest a little and let its ever-present and anxiety driven clinched-fist guard down.

The more facts the mind holds in its archives and the more it has access to them, the safer the false self feels and the more it believes its survival as a body-mind-identity depends on its ability to navigate safely through the dangerous waters of the grand illusion … as it sees it.

Skills, talents and special abilities are highly regarded and sought after … even revered and worshipped in some cultures offering those who possess them an extra degree of comfort and security.

However, the specter of *what-ifs* constantly haunts the false self who knows well that what it has, can be taken away from its fearful and tenuous grasp at any moment. It knows that a shift in health, a freak accident, an unforeseen governmental or economic crisis can instantly collapse a fortress of security that took a lifetime to establish.

The massive global presence of the insurance industry is one example of the pervasive fear that stalks even the most securely provided-for false self. There is no magical panacea formula that guarantees the safety of the fragile false self's existence no matter how great the expansion of technological wonders the world achieves.

What is NOT Real is no more secure than a passing cloud destined soon for desolation. This too is a persistent thorn in the side that drives the sleeping God-SELF *inward*.

It is through its tricks and seductions that the body-mind-identity attempts to keep you from a full-scale rebellion … until, when you have finally had enough, and you are exhausted and fed up, you turn within and ask for help from the only Source that can lead you HOME. In this way Life *uses* the grand dream *to dream you out of* the trap you have long been imprisoned within.

Chapter Five

THE CHANGING DREAM- *DESCENT*

During the *Descent* of the Awareness of Who You Really Are, the false self dominates the world dream. As such, competition, conflict and chaos has subtly surrounded the tiniest interactions and overtly swept across the world through *power* and *control* struggles in an attempt to grasp the limited resources the collective false self believes defines its illusionary reality.

What it calls happiness has been oriented in some way to *conquest* and much of it is related to the pride of vanquishing what it believes are its enemies, which it perceives to be everyone and everything ... *in some way*. Its relationship to a higher power [if any] has always been associated with bargaining, cajoling and when necessary, even begging in some way.

No matter what mask it has worn – a conquering perpetrator to a subservient victim, the simmering stench of fear has always been its constant companion. These have been the story/dramas on the stage of the grand dream for countless eons ... until recently.

Now, the *Descent* of Awareness has interfaced with the *Awakening* Phase.

PART TWO

AWAKENING

The Doldrums

MASS AWAKENING

There is a swirling mass of Awakening sweeping away everything that is stuck, entrenched in the time and space restricted belief systems of limitation found in the ancient energies that have now faded and will soon dissolve completely. The feeling that accompanies this Divine maelstrom is of possibilities. It is subtle but speaks of a Life that is grander than humanity has allowed itself to believe ... until NOW.

It may suppress this 'hint' of grandeur but the 'essence' of it grows daily as it senses Life is somehow 'vast' yet right here and NOW. It has been rehearsing for this show forever and now the stage-lights have come on and the chairs are filled, the music plays its cacophonous warm up and as ONE it waits in the wings about to make an entrance.

INTRODUCTION

There are many millions who have entered the *Awakening phase* where, on some level, they have realized that the world is a dream. This is *NOT* Freedom ... but it is the beginning of *the Awareness of its possibility* although the tendency exists that they may believe they have so-called - *arrived.*

At this turning point there is a very *sticky net* to keep you ensnared within its clutches that the false self uses because its deception has been *discovered* and it must retreat deeper within the shadows of illusion now that you know that it is NOT who you are.

On the *Ascent-turn* toward the full Awareness of the God You Are the heavy load of *conditioning,* which includes mental baggage, and all learned spiritual knowledge, must be released [transformed] as the steep climb HOME to Freedom *consciously* begins.

Until one is willing to *stand in the fire* of all deeply hidden programs [conditioning] and really FEEL them … staying in them until they subside, they are just *playing with Freedom,* peering out through the bars mumbling to themselves … *"someday".*

At the beginning of Awakening, many are living in a somewhat *smoother* dream world where everything seems wonderful and blissful and heavenly while the stench of their still hidden conditioning is band-aided whenever and wherever it dares to peak through the cracks of their now, rose-colored Awareness.

Now is the Moment when all who still hang onto the tattered shreds of *control* and the illusion of maintaining some kind of *personal identity,* to *open fully* to whatever comes up. Scream if need be, swear, rage, pound fists but be fearless and *open fully,* regardless of consequences.

Real Freedom is a *jealous lover* and will not tolerate any coveted desires whether they be dark and repulsive or smelling of the sugary sweetness of secret passions - all must be burned up in this *transforming* fire.

Ask Yourself

"Is what I am thinking, speaking and doing leading to my absolute Freedom in some way?"

Other than providing for the *bare essentials*, why would you engage in anything else? Since there *is* only *one* WILL [free will exists only as a dream within the dream world of a separated identity where it seems very real indeed]. Everything ultimately leads toward a return to the full Awareness of Who You Really Are ... but the circuitous route most choose can be a very, very long journey.

Measured in the timeless realm of Pure Conscious Awareness this return took no time nor did the *Descent* from this Awareness ... *IT just IS*. However, while one is dreaming, time seems a very real factor. When you have arrived [so-called] at the *Awakened* state of recognizing you have been sleeping to Truth, you *can* immediately choose absolute Freedom as your only *focus*. And this undivided Attention *will* draw you HOME very quickly.

But if you choose the false self's trick of *trying to save the world* and *the rest of sleeping humanity*, you have chosen a new dream, far more insidious and covert than the illusion that the dream world and universe are. It is a miasma of pitfalls laden with *special-ness and subtle arrogance* that binds your *awakened state* within a gilded cage as a beautiful trapped bird. The cage is larger than the one you just left, and the bars are further away so that you cannot see them easily but make no mistake, your priestly robes, no matter of what discipline or practice you lean toward ... are chains binding you to a different, now candy-coated prison.

There is no greater help you can give to the sleeping masses then your own *Real Freedom*, which radiates out to the entire dream universe effortlessly and invisibly touching every Heart. The one who *stands in Truth* is like a *blazing sun* compared to a flickering candle no matter how beautiful the candle-stick it rests in.

Nevertheless, *if you are drawn to some service to humanity* while your Attention is focused on your own absolute Freedom and it has been filtered through the lens of Joy and therefore resonates with your Heart ... then *for a season,* this too is part of your return HOME. *Massaging the dream* so that it is *directed* more toward the *discovery* of Who You Really Are, does have value.

But let no *attachment* or *identification* shackle your resolve. If you cannot let it go *in an instant* without remorse, then it is a trick of the false self.

To change the world is not your business

To change yourself is not your duty

To awaken to your True SELF is your opportunity

The greatest healing is to wake up to what you are NOT

- Mooji

Chapter One

AWAKENING

There are many *symptoms* of Awakening that have been written about and as a reference you will find a section in the *prequel* to this book "YOU ARE GOD" that goes into a fair amount of detail on the subject. However, as a very brief thumbnail sketch here are a few symptoms:

-Caring less and less about what people think of you

-Craving simplicity

-Losing interest in life events that once captivated your attention

-Things that do interest you show up without effort

-Many friends and family members drift away

-Your body goes through many unexplainable changes that usually come and go quickly

If you are reading this book you have already and will continue to experience many symptoms of shifting *from the Descent* into Un-consciousness of Who you Really Are that prevails within the grand dream and are either in the *turnstile of Awakening* or have *begun the Ascent* back into Full Consciousness of your True SELF.

The Turning Point

When one has reached the last rung of the ladder of *Descent* where the Awareness of Who They Really Are has completely engulfed them in the mists of illusion, the world they have called reality appears its darkest and most hopeless. No bright smile, encouraging words or shifts from so-called bad to good circumstances registers the possibility of a better life and a simmering depression mixed with bitterness, anger and hatred for everything is their constant companion. The evidence of this is widespread in the varying degrees of unspeakable acts the false self identity is capable of when it feels like a trapped and abused animal.

It may be very difficult to realize that beneath this dark and ugly mask the pristine Beauty of the God You/All Are, dwells. You chose to experience *all* possibilities in the grand dream and this extreme swing of the pendulum illustrates this blatantly.

For the one that has arrived at this level of *Unconsciousness,* it is likely that the body they are wearing is also mirroring this level of *awareness* in many challenging ways exhibiting a variety of health challenges. At this point Life is truly a miserable experience and some will choose to end it by their own hands or by placing themselves in harm's way, only to return again and again in similar circumstances until finally the inevitable line in the sand is reached where the magical question is asked in some way,

"There must be a better way."

For some this question may seem to come to them quickly and easily but we do not know how many times that one has been at *the end of their rope* to bring them, in this lifetime, to the great *turn inward* toward Truth.

For many, that turn has not initially been *inward* where Truth resides but has been influenced by an endless menu of ways and means *out there* that involved enormous effort and a great swath of time. These are the multitude of modalities, disciplines and practices that so-called *seekers* have taken up in their *search* for Truth and Freedom.

There have been no lack of leaders, priests, gurus and counselors ready and waiting to lead eager followers through a maze of *How-To's* toward the promised Self-Realization they offer. But not one has ever attained Freedom through *seeking out there* because out there only the grand dream exists, disguised to seekers as the way HOME.

However, they *have* served the purpose of bringing many to the door that leads inward but as Rumi put it:

"I have lived on the lip of insanity, wanting to know reasons, knocking on a door. It opens. I've been knocking from the inside".

There is no door, no secret and definitely *no path* [the very word suggests time and space, the original cause of separation and the fall of Consciousness]. All seeking, paths and modalities keep you chasing your tail and places Freedom out in the future where it does NOT exist. They do however bring you to total exhaustion where it becomes possible to recognize that *you are already Free*, you *are* already and have always been What you are seeking.

You only need to shift your *Attention* away from the grand dream, which includes *seeking* toward the Truth You already Are. *Attention on* Truth has always been the *direct pathless-path* Home, hidden in plain sight. But the false-self-identity has been your constant companion on the long and arduous false *path* to no-where, disguised <u>as</u> your friend and ally. *"It seeks but never finds"* [paraphrasing ACIM] because to find the True SELF the false-self-identity must lose its usurped throne as the identity you call *myself.*

This is the real death all sleepers fear.

The SELF then resumes its rightful role, crowned again as the Conscious Awareness of the God-SELF You Are. It has *never been gone or lost*, only forgotten as your Attention was placed on the grand dream of *littleness, limitation* and *separation* and that Attention, focused for eons on this illusion made it seem a rock-solid reality.

Attention combined with *Passion* and *Activity* manifested every experience you have ever had as the sleeping God-SELF seemingly separated throughout numberless entities.

Listening

Long before the simple Awakened Awareness that the Life you have been living is NOT the Real Life, dawns upon you, the sleeping God-SELF You Are receives a steady unbroken stream of inner guidance. Since before that, ITs Attention is focused entirely *out there*, the small amount of this guidance that IT does hear [as the false self it is portraying] is placed under the obscure and questionable headings of *gut feelings* and *hunches*.

Later, the brief flashes that it becomes Aware of may be referred to as *women's intuition*, usually with at least a hint of distain particularly if it occurs in a male. When Awakening occurs the list of inner guidance references expands to include, *insights, visions,* and the *still-small-voice* and in spiritual circles is spoken of with respect … even reverence and is often treated as special, sometimes referred to as various *psychic abilities.*

And yet IT is simply Pure Conscious Awareness speaking to the *now awakening* God-SELF *IT is* through thinner and thinner veils of conditioning as the spiraling arc of the *Descent* of Consciousness makes the turn into an *Ascent* toward Freedom. As this *Ascent* continues some will label the voice as *spirit guides, personal angels, extra-terrestrials, channeled masters* and many other terms that continue to suggest the *externalization* of ONE-ness. ONE is always ONE and speaks only to IT SELF no matter how it *seems* to show up. This seemingly tiny distinction continues to foster separation, which the false self endorses.

The resistance to accepting that You as the God-SELF are simply speaking to YOUR/IT SELF, is greater than facing any other conditioning that defines the false self. The reason is because more than anything, this *triggers* the root conditioning - *unworthiness*. When one begins to focus their Attention steadfastly on Who They Really Are, even while it is still only an intellectual concept, the Truth of it *expands* until it becomes an unbroken Awareness experience, which *is* HOME - IT SELF.

This is why *declaring* Who You Really Are is the direct route HOME and will very quickly expose all the conditioning that is blocking the Truth and keeping you locked in limitation as the false-self-identity.

I AM or *I AM That I AM* are simple ways to make this declaration of Truth. For me, it was *I AM Freedom*. Whatever resonates with you is fine as long as you *add nothing* to the simple word you place after I AM, which would diminish its strength. For example, I AM Love, I AM Beauty, I AM Peace, etc.

The one thing to recognize early on is that you are *always* being shown *where to go, what to do, what to say* and *to whom* and *what you need to know in each moment*. When you begin to genuinely *listen*, the feeling of *aloneness* that plagues the false self begins to dissolve.

The question does arise sooner or later, *"How do I know that I am hearing the Real voice of Truth?"* The answer is, simply filter what you are receiving through the lens of JOY and you will instantly know.

Chapter Two

Stuck In Awakening

When you enter the *turnstile* out of the *Descent* of Conscious Awareness into the grand dream, which turns toward the *Ascent* back to the Conscious Awareness of Who You Really Are the false self's tactics to maintain its identity as who you believe you are becomes very subtle. It *has* been exposed but must retain credibility or you will very quickly dive inward where Truth resides.

Its new profile is as your best friend and proclaims itself as *you - Awakened,* suggesting through that new identity badge that you are now *somehow Free* ... even *subtly exalted* in some special way. The opportunity for the false self to *expand* the *separated Consciousness* that has kept the sleeping God-SELF imprisoned is now *even greater* and can remain hidden for the rest of one's lifetime because you may still be looking *out there*, but this time as a *would-be-savior* to the still sleeping lost world.

There is an insidious and almost invisible kind of *arrogance* that presents itself through this new-found spiritual Awareness and depending on how large your spiritual archive of information may be, many will be impressed and even dazzled by what you present as your new-and-improved world view.

Many alternatively will be intimidated by your *certainty* about how Life works and this, often more than the adoring cheering crowds of aspirants, newbies and toe-dippers into the spiritual world, can expand your sense of individual empowerment through a defiant and resolute attitude, further separating you from the rest of humanity. I was one of these types of *special awakened ones* [so I thought] for over two decades.

I had been an effective communicator all my life and up until 1999 when I took the NO MATTER WHAT plunge into Self Discovery this ability more than any other had given me significant wealth, influence, security and fame within the industry I was in. I used this gift very effectively in the spiritual community to convince people that I had some *special* knowledge and the one fooled by the validation I received, more than anyone, was me ... that is, the *new me* I thought was.

When one has *Truly become Aware* of Who They Really Are they will likely still have identification instruments such as a passport, birth certificate, driver's license and bank cards but the name on these identity instruments will only be a name and NOT Who you *KNOW* Your SELF to BE.

Another aspect of the *savior complex* that often affects the newly Awakened seeker involves *causes.* There are no shortage of causes to support within the grand dream. As the Light of Truth expands it exposes more and more of the collapsing house of cards the false self has manifested for eon upon eon. The new technologies the world now possesses allows for instant communication and fans the flames of outrage in numberless ways about how bad the state of the world is ... or so the collective false self believes.

What the now *yawning-awakened one* cannot see is that the world *cannot be fixed* ... because it's a dream and has manifested through the illusion of time and space, which in turn generates the illusion of separation. No matter how many changes are made to it, the energy of separation will pop up somewhere else *often* disguised as something totally different.

What the *Truly Free one* experiences while living IN the grand dream but not OF it is the Light of Love and Beauty that flows within the veins of the temporary projections that constantly come and go within the playground of the dream. This cannot be *believed into* or *thought into* one's experience ... you must be *Truly Free* to experience this. Its not an intellectual experience, *it's a state of Being.*

Nevertheless, there are many *yawning-awakened ones* that claim they experience this, and this is when the false self *has really got control* of its fake identity.

If you are moved to become involved in one or more of the many causes to change this or that and after *authentically* filtering this inspiration through the lens of Joy, the feeling still persists, then that is where you are supposed to be ... *for now.* Every Intention to bring relief and happiness to humanity and the world in general, despite the conditioning that these intentions still flow through, all *point* in the direction of actual Freedom, but this route can be a very long road HOME indeed.

> *All paths*
> *lead to Self Inquiry*
> *...into Liberation*
> -Ramana

Talking To God

The false self uses very subtle ways to keep you as the individuated sleeping God-SELF, *imprisoned* in the grand dream. The way you speak to the God You Are can be a very powerful influence to help Free you from this bondage.

If, for example you are engaged in prayer it is common to communicate *as if* you are speaking *to* God. The beauty and serenity of this practice makes it easy to fall into this delicate trap. You *Are* God-ONE. There is nothing but ONE Consciousness and you Are IT. Just the mere suggestion of this can immediately arouse an uncomfortable feeling that may be thought of as blasphemous if you have a religious background or at the very least feel incredibly arrogant.

"How can I be God?"

... the false self will protest. How can you NOT be God if there is *nothing else*? Few have really gone deeply into the simplicity of this question, which easily registers as True when *felt* rather than *thought* about. ONE is always ONE.

A *tiny shift* in your language can dissolve the ancient program that keeps this separation-oriented communication alive. If you said, *"Show me what I need to know for my highest Purpose Great Spirit"* [or whatever name for God you prefer], then added – *I AM* after the name you are using for God, you are acknowledging that you are speaking *to* Your SELF *as* God.

Even if you are expressing *gratitude* for something it is still You *as* God, you are thanking. *"Thank you God – I AM, for this beautiful day"* is a simple expression that declares You *as* God are thanking Your SELF. It's a tiny shift but makes a *huge dent* in the deeply entrenched belief in the separation that is the original cause behind the grand dream as well as all suffering.

It is not sufficient to *intellectually* speak of and believe that you are God, the conditioning that has held you captive for lifetimes must be *transformed* back into the nothing-ness from which it arose. This kind of repeated acknowledgement will *trigger* the conditioning that keeps the belief in a separated God in place and allow it to be transformed. When the conditioned belief in separation has been transformed, the Real You *is* Free.

Chapter Three

WHO IS THIS NEW "I"

"Tell me what to do, where to go, what to say, who to say it to and what I need to know."

Who Is This "I" that asks for help and guidance? At first it is the false self - acting as a conduit for the SELF to connect to ITs sleeping individuated God-SELF imprisoned beneath the false-self-identity you call myself.

During many eons and lifetimes, the false-self-identity reaches a multitude of impasses where it cannot control its life experience. In Truth ALL control is an illusion, but the false self believes it has varying degrees of control and when it arrives at roadblocks it cannot overcome, it asks for help.

Depending on its particular conditioning it may ask for this help from some God it believes exists outside itself or perhaps through some superior power it feels exists elsewhere or in others ... there are many sources it may call on for help.

Usually there will be some bargaining and or begging involved as this is how it believes its world functions and hopes that the unseen powers that be [if they exist], may work the same way.

Eventually, usually many lifetimes, the answers or help it receives fail to deliver results that satisfy, and the false self's attempts at trying to control life diminishes to the point that a breakthrough occurs that provides a key to the dungeon where the True God-SELF has resided – sleeping, since the Descent of Consciousness.

The prison represents the conditioning that acts as a barrier hiding the Light of the SELF, which blocks the Awareness of the individuated God-SELF within the body-mind ... from IT SELF. In these breakthrough moments direct communication is possible between the sleeping God-SELF and the fully Consciousness SELF. They are both ONE and the same entity but seem separate due to the illusion of separation the false self has solidified through its conditioned illusionary identity.

This is what many call surrender and it is an on again off again experience since the false self, for a long time, returns to its usurped throne once life seems to get back to its version of normal, which has become an acceptable dysfunctional experience. Typically, when it reaches this level of acceptance it can be heard saying: "Well, that's just how life works," and that resignation may last for lifetimes.

Finally, a moment comes when the false self is so totally frustrated with its life experience that surrender becomes a repetitive experience. This opens the way for genuine Self Discovery to begin and the conditioning that has defined the false self to be transformed back into the nothing-ness from which it arose.

As this occurs the Light of Truth, which is the Real SELF, shines through to the Now Awakened and Ascending God-SELF more and more until the Awareness of ONE-ness returns. **Nothing has changed at all** … only the Awareness of Truth [what already IS] has expanded. When one has truly and fully surrendered, this New 'I' that is speaking, and acting is the Consciously Aware God-SELF.

The collective false self will say that the body cannot be used to navigate the dream without it, but there is no better captain of that ship than the God-SELF now in unbroken touch with the Real SELF through total surrender.

When Jesus said, while standing at the opened tomb of Lasarus, *"Father, I know that you have always heard me ..."* He Knew that He, as a Consciously Aware individuated God-SELF, was speaking to Him-SELF as God.

Chapter Four

MIND THOUGHT
HEART FEELINGS

The mind or false-self-body-mind-identity is *a made-up entity* most call *myself.* The sleeping God-SELF has been convinced over and over again that the false self *is* ITs True identity, and most cannot imagine an existence without it. And yet it is nothing but *conditioning* [attachments, expectations and identifications tied to memory]. When the end of this false self's existence becomes a possibility a dynamic *survival instinct* is triggered.

It will feign sincerity that it is seeking Freedom and become involved in all manner of research on the subject but if it gets *too close to the fire of Truth* it will use every trick it has to avoid Freedom, which would mean its demise.

The loss of a *personal identity* IS this death. The body-mind-identity, in its usurped role as who you are, uses tens of thousands of thoughts each day to navigate within the grand dream of separation … most are the same thoughts insuring that whatever they are will remain a part of its existence. As stated already, focused *Attention* is the conduit through which *Life-Force* flows and *manifests* within the dream.

This is why *stilling the mind* has had so much attention as an instrument leading to Freedom. *"Still the mind and the Light of Truth will appear."* This is True. However, the *thought* of stilling the mind *IS still thinking*. Nevertheless, if this route to Freedom, when filtered through the lens of Joy resonates with you, it *is* for you.

The Heart or God-SELF functions through Feelings or Knowing [when it is Conscious] and has no past or future archives sticking to it to *offer ideas, opinions* or *concepts* … IT simply IS. The *shift* from *mind-thoughts* to *Heart-Feelings* occurs on its own automatically when your Attention is placed only on Truth. You do NOT need to know what Truth IS and indeed the false-self-body-mind-identity is not capable of understanding what IT is.

Only your simple Attention *on* Truth by any name will expand the Light [Awareness] of IT. *Freedom, Peace, Joy, Love, Abundance, Beauty,*

God, the SELF, I AM and other names are all interchangeable names for *Truth.* Freedom was the word I preferred. As the Light expands due to the Life-Force flowing through your focused Attention, whatever has been blocking [the conditioning that defines your false self], your Awareness of IT will then be *triggered.*

For those who resist this shift, these vignettes will occur usually through pain and suffering generated through stories and dramas. For those who consciously pursue Truth, more gentle ways and means will often illustrate what conditioning is ready to be transformed. For example, a *flash of insight,* a *sign* or a *symbol* may point you toward what conditioning is arising to be transformed.

As the Truth expands more and more the *thoughts* you once used to navigate the grand dream will be replaced by *Heart-Feelings* that contain no grey areas and always point you HOME to Freedom.

Letting Go

In order to shift *from* the *Awakened* state, which is the *Awareness of the possibility of Freedom* to the actual Awareness of the God-SELF you Are, *letting go completely* must occur. This means all *control, all beliefs, all definitions* and *all history must* be released, and all individual *decisions* and *choices* must be handed over to the now Awakening Sleeping Beauty God-SELF.

In the *un-awakened* state everything that can be explained to the mind from *out there*, no matter how wise or beautiful it may seem, is *compared* to *where it believes it is* at the moment and that judgment holds Awareness in *littleness* and *unworthiness.* It literally freezes it in place because the size of the undertaking to go from *here* to *there,* from the tiny individual to the infinite Being-ness of Who You Really Are seems far-too much for it to fathom as a possibility. And this is usually well beneath its Conscious radar.

When one has been Awakened, there is a much more expanded view and yet that very opening can mask the conditioning that still defines a separated false-self-identity. As already outlined, this is a very delicate stage. As stated, what can happen is that the false self takes on a new disguised identity as a *special Awakened one* and there the imprisoned SELF remains until complete *letting go* takes place.

Chapter Five

THE CHANGING DREAM - *AWAKENING*

In the last 100+ years of the grand dream [within the illusion of time], the influence of expanding communication, at vastly increased speeds, has made it possible to shine a bright Light on deceit ... instantly. All manner of ancient and recent subterfuge and hidden agendas have been exposed and this has fostered the expansion of Awareness.

The questioning that has arisen from this expanded *vision* has led to the *Awakening* phase that now interfaces the dissolving *Descent* phase. Many millions have now shifted out of the cloistered existence of the complete blindness of the sleeping God-SELF and into the *prison-courtyard* where the Light of Truth is shining and pointing Consciousness toward ITs True HOME.

Sleeping Beauty has been kissed and is beginning to rouse out of her long and deep slumber. In this *intermediary* phase there is a tendency to try to *fix the world* since the slowly Awakening God-SELF does not yet realize a dream *cannot be fixed.* The most IT can do is rearrange *the conditioned energy of the illusion.*

Many newly awakened ones become trapped in this well-intentioned cycle while others [there really *are* no others] attempt to use spirituality to feather-the-bed of their *new dream* and slip into a cozy stupor of on-again-off-again bliss.

To the few who rise from their slumber and choose absolute Freedom NO MATTER WHAT, the *fire of who they are NOT* awaits and HOME now draws very near.

PART THREE

THE ASCENT

The Upward Spiral

YOU ARE NOT

You are not your imagination, fantasies or dreams
You are not your memories, desires or hopes
You are not your anxieties, sorrow or fears
You are not your remorse, guilt or shame
You are not the ugliness you perceive and judge
You are not your thoughts, nor what they create
You are not your body, mind or emotions
You are not your attachments, expectations or identities

All these things and many more rise and fall, wave after wave, unique as snowflakes, here for a season, brief or seemingly eternal yet appearing then dissolving.

Nothing 'real' comes and goes.

That which comes and goes are toys in your playground, there for your enjoyment but not to hold onto. YOU alone ARE. There 'is' only ONE and everything you can experience abides within YOU as a projection on the screen of Consciousness.

There is nothing else but YOU and yet you are 'nothing', empty, creating dreams to experience yourself through. It is your attachment to these dreams that causes your suffering ... nothing else.

Attention on YOU or ONE ... call it God or I AM or what you will, withdraws attention on these ephemeral dreams until only ONE is known as REAL. At first you will waffle back and forth between these seductive temporary appearances and ONE but be not disturbed ... the echoes of your ancient dreams WILL fade as you fix your gaze steadily on WHO you really ARE ... as your Grandeur and Beauty undresses before your **Ascending' Awareness.**

INTRODUCTION

IT'S ALL FOR YOU

Your world is *All For You*. It is a unique expression on the screen of Consciousness, *which* You, as *Pure Conscious Awareness* animate in order to experience Your SELF. It's All You because there *is* only ONE, ONE Consciousness. At the moment you may only be Aware of Consciousness within the body that you are wearing. And yet, it *is* likely that you have experienced Your SELF as another aspect of Consciousness.

The *personal identity* that most consider themselves to be, may temporarily dissolve, lost in a moment in which you are deeply passionate. It could be as simple as a beloved hobby or as intense as a rapturous piece of music. Neither is somehow *better* than the other, it is simply felt in varying degrees of passion.

When you are Truly Free [that is, Aware of the Freedom that You Are], it will be just as normal for you to experience Life in the body you are currently occupying as it will to be ONE *as* the consciousness of your pet cat or a flower or an entire garden, a whole city or a snowflake that just landed on your nose. All are YOU at various levels of Conscious Awareness of Who You Really Are.

This illustrates part of the motive behind your projection of the universe. None of this sticks however ... You *as* the Freedom You Are do NOT identify with these temporary experiences of Consciousness beyond your body. You enjoy each moment then let them go and move on.

In matters of romantic relationships for example, one may say, *"I can't live without you. You are my reason for living."* This confines Consciousness to a very small Life experience that at the moment may feel like your entire world. Some have this same reaction to possessions as simple as a beloved automobile or a house. Or the confinement may be tied to a business, a country or a global cause of some sort.

There are many manifestations and experiences that narrow Consciousness down to a tiny state in an impossible attempt to *place a frame around the infinite Life* You Are. For a season, it can seem this has happened. Most of humanity has experienced this to some extent for eons. But Life *cannot be confined* indefinitely and eventually the seams split and the illusion collapses.

This is the nature of the grand dream as it shifts and changes in an unbroken thread of *birth, expression* and *death*. Only that which has no birth or death [the unborn] is Real and this is a simple way to recognize what really matters. It is not the sunset that matters but the *Beauty* [another word for Who You Really Are] *within* the sunset that touches your Heart and fills you up. The sunset is transient while Beauty is eternal.

The Heart *refers to* the individuated God-SELF as an expression of the ONE SELF. Always Life is speaking to Life. The instruments that it utilizes to do this are no more important than the piano or violin that you use to express music through. The music is *always* Present and the God-SELF You Are *uses* your body and the musical instrument to express it.

Of course, celebrate the body and the craftsmanship of the musical instruments but then let them go. If you attach yourself to them … then you are placing invisible chains around the God-SELF.

Finally, *Ascending* is like the *twilight* when you are emerging slowly from a deep sleep in the morning. You are a little bit there and a little bit here, without a point of reference to ground you to one of the other. This is why those who are *Ascending* often seem *disoriented.*

Chapter One

ASCENDING

As related earlier, the universe is a projection on the screen of Consciousness of the Light that IT/YOU are, coalesced into various levels of compression so that the appearance of *manifestation* occurs through the application of ***Attention, Passion and Activity.***

All this, including your body appears [is born] then dissolves [dies] in cycles that repeat endlessly until the sleeping God-SELF that You Are turns from this grand illusion toward ITs inward journey HOME to the Awareness of Who IT Really Is [*Ascends*]. **This is NOT really *a journey*** since there is nowhere to go. Only the illusions of time and space and separation makes it seem that there is a path from here to there.

Everything is *preordained,* the entire universe, the world and your experience navigating through it ... ***has already happened*** described in the *Tapestry* metaphor passage a little later. All this is the playground of the God-ONE that We All Are. Many speak of creating or co-creating their reality but *manifesting what already IS, is what is occurring.*

You as God – ONE *are* the Consciousness within every aspect of the grand dream, this includes everyone who has ever incarnated anywhere [not just on Earth] and this is how every possible outcome or circumstance within the preordained nature of the dream can be experienced.

For example, if you are deeply immersed in the belief in separation and therefore believe you are an individual, then this false-self-identity believes it is firmly *in control* … whether it is *efficient* in that false role is not the point, it believes it is alone in the world and must make its own way totally through its own initiatives. This is the *opposite* of *going with the flow* of Life.

As a result, the Perfect and preordained route through your incarnation is constantly at odds with this false self's desires and with the ways and means it is using to *try* to make its desires happen. This is the way the vast majority live their lives and as such they endure *enormous* amounts of *chaos, conflict* and *suffering*. Going with the flow is *as the crow flies* and going it on your own is a zig-zag route filled with detours and pitfalls.

Every conceivable possibility exists within the grand dream and as the false-self-identity flounders while it *goes its own way*, many possibilities that *were meant for you* are missed. However, as the ONE Consciousness, you WILL experience everything so-called missed through another false self [since there are no others]. In this way it is not possible for Consciousness to miss anything that IT preordained for IT SELF to experience.

The unmanifested Life experience is *felt*…. for some, very clearly through Visions much like Mozart received his musical compositions - *full blown* and *all at once*. For most however, it seems like Life is just happening *to* them, NOT *of* them as an aspect of Who They Really Are.

What they are doing is *tracing* already created outlines holographically. Where you go, what you do, what you *seem to create* … how it all plays out is already played out before you ever experience it. If you go with the flow, meaning as the God-SELF devoid of all conditioning, the pen of manifestation is effortless, but for most and for eons the sense of personal doer-ship generates a knee-jerk movement of the pen and many detours are taken bringing with them the inevitable suffering that separation brings with the belief in victims.

These detours are also part of the infinite choices preordained ... every possibility is played out by some aspect of the sleeping God-SELF, Who is ONE.

Eventually, when this made-up individual identity is *exhausted* with its endless attempts to *make-life-happen* its way ... surrendering into this effortless tracing-manifestation of What-Is, takes place. When this takes place, *Life is Living You [Ascending]*, that is, Life [as Who You Really Are] is Living IT SELF unimpeded by the limited separated body-mind-identity that you have been calling yourself.

Chapter Two

THE COSTUME

To navigate within the grand dream you must wear a costume ... a body that seems to move from here to there across a vast and ever shifting landscape beginning with a world and extending into endless universes. To accomplish this, you require an operating system for this body-costume, which is handled flawlessly by Consciousness if not interfered with. However, the conditioning which defines the false self *does interfere* and all manner of dysfunctions occur within the body as a result.

As stated before, in order for the deception of the grand dream to manifest there must also be the illusion of time and space, which seems to divide ONE-ness into numberless pieces. Manifestation cannot occur without this impression of separation. One must *appear* separated.

When the Real You awakens fully to the ONE it *is*, that All That Is *is*, the delusion of separation has gone. Those who have realized the Truth and been Freed from the bondage of the delusion of separation, usually do not linger within the dream. They soon depart the costume-body and return *fully* to the ONE Consciousness from which all that seems to be arose.

However, for those who do choose to remain for a while, the body disguise is required, and that entity will still have the appearance of a unique individual. For those who have known the entity prior to its *Ascension* it may seem that that one is still the same so-called person. However, that person no longer exists despite the presence of a similar, albeit *glowing essence.*

What still appears is a costume, now operated by Pure Conscious Awareness, untouched by the conditioning that once defined a seemingly separated individual. This one may be referred to as a *master* and display some of the same idiosyncrasies as its previous tenant, but the tenant no longer exists as the conditioning that once defined it has dissolved.

This is your destiny and **has already occurred**, and yet nothing is really happening in a dream … another Divine Dichotomy.

The Tapestry

Imagine a tiny insect crawling along a maze of threads of every tone and color, each with its own energy signature that represents the stories and dramas within the grand dream. Some twist and turn while others ascend and descend changing and morphing as the insect crawls along amongst the maze of threads.

The insect experiences many obstacles and unimaginable swings from one extreme to another. It tries to find an easy way in and out of the tangled world it cannot understand but as it exercises more and more effort, the going seems to become increasingly more complicated and difficult.

One day it encounters a similar looking insect with wings who is capable of rising up and out of the web of threads the crawling insect calls life. The winged insect explains that the world the crawling insect is experiencing is ONE and that in Reality that ONE is beautiful beyond description. It goes on to say that it is visiting other crawling insects to tell them of this Truth but very few believe what they hear.

The crawling insect is told that it too possesses wings and that they are closer than close but that it must look beneath the hard insect shell it wears to find them, not hidden but in plain view tucked away waiting to be used. It simply needs to give its *Attention* to them and that focus will bring them into sight. These wings represent Awareness.

The crawling insect is told that when it makes this shift of Attention away from the tangled web and toward its wings, very soon it will find itself flying up and away where it will recognize that what it believed was a harsh and cruel environment is really an exquisite and beautiful tapestry, perfect in every way.

The crawling insect is told that in that instant the tapestry will be seen for *what it really is*, and the insect will shed the shell of littleness and limitation it falsely wears.

Chapter Three

THE MANY FACES OF TRUTH

L IFE is like a diamond with a multitude of facets, each representing a different aspect of IT SELF. *Love, Freedom, Peace, Abundance, Joy* and *Beauty* are frequencies that seem to stand alone and yet are ONE *as* Life not *with* Life which would immediately act like a partner to Life but therefore be separate … Life is ONE.

Life does not *have* these aspects since this too is separation and as with the false-self-identity, what it *has* can be taken away. Life *is* these aspects and can never *not* BE them. What you *are* IS and is never NOT.

The many gods and goddesses in the Hindu religion represent these aspects of Life or the ONE God. They have been [and for many still are] useful concepts for the sleeping God-SELF to focus Its Attention upon and thereby bring alive in Its Awakening experience, but they DO give the appearance of being *outside* and in this way can foster the illusion of separation, the very cause behind Its sleep.

If they resonate with you when filtered through the lens of Joy then for the present moment they are part of your Awakening. However, the SELF *has no beliefs of any kind* and at some point, all beliefs must be put aside in favor of *NOT knowing,* which is the conduit for *spontaneous Knowing* when the need arises to Know.

This is part of the simplicity of the God-SELF, the Life You Are, eliminating the heavy burden of accumulated knowledge, which the false self embraces and wears like a merit badge.

As your Awareness *Ascends* toward the Pure Conscious Awareness that You Are many of the *aspects* of the ONE God You Are will *expand* as well ... some more than others according to what you most resonate with. For example, *Freedom* was my chief *focus* while my Awareness first began to *Ascend* out of the grand dream but Now it is *Love,* which I find myself sinking deeper and deeper into as the Expansion of the I AM Presence continues ... a *never-ending* experience and yet still *timeless.*

Remember, these expressions *are* YOU ... you don't *have* them. I call these the *Many Faces of*

Life and as they expand in your Awareness you will recognize them as *Ascension symptoms.*

Love

The Love the false self speaks so eloquently about, in numberless ways since the original *Descent* of the Consciousness of Who You Really Are, is NOT Love as stated earlier. The false self is made up of conditioning and as such the concept of *Unconditional Love* is not possible no matter how much the body-mind-identity speaks of it.

Every thought, word and deed associated with the outward expression of Love is colored and tainted by the unique conditioning of each false self, which *always places itself first* in the grand dream of separation and the competitiveness that arises out of this belief.

As mentioned, there are instances when the false self may for a moment be temporarily sublimated such as in the midst of an exquisite piece if music or a magnificent Nature setting, and in that moment an *epiphany* may take place that takes that one into the Conscious Awareness of Truth. There, Unconditional Love may be experienced, however for most their conditioning will quickly draw them back into the grand dream again. However, such *Truth vignettes* can never be forgotten and act as a powerful magnet for the *upward Ascent* all will eventually make.

When Love is Un-Conditioned you are Aware that the Real You – Consciousness, is the same Consciousness *in* everyone [in everything]. Then, you are allowing this aspect of YOU to experience and express IT SELF ... as *IT* chooses, without interference of any kind, such as what occurs through the control-games that are so common in *false-self-relationships* of any kind.

The deep longing the sleeping God-SELF has to reunite with ITs fully Conscious SELF [seemingly separated yet still ONE] flows through every imitating expression of Love and as such is a blend of True and false. For many, this becomes their *way* Home as they make attempt after attempt to express the *expanding* moments they are having of genuine Love. Many great artists have explained their intense angst in trying to put down through pen or ink or paint or express through sculpture, poetry or prose the deep sense of ONE-ness they were having as Love pulled them *inward* and *upward*.

Occasionally photos have been taken of fully Self Realized beings that show clearly the essence of genuine Love, such as the last image of Yogananda prior to him leaving his body.

In the Presence of un-conditioned Love [an Enlightened Being], you may feel a sense of tranquility where the guards that the false self always have up, fall away. This *Pure-environment* can actually create an *opening* in your own sleeping God-SELF to radiate – OUT *of* You Who You Really Are. It is YOU that is emanating Love *through* YOU to your world. This is your Natural state of Being.

Peace

Peace is spoken of even more than is Love, perhaps due to the widespread and continuous conflicts constantly occurring throughout the grand dream. It is where the *field of dreams* finds its greatest fertility as the mind offers endless solutions together with a multitude of ways and means for the body-mind-identity to engage itself in distracting you from the core of YOU, which is *Peace* IT SELF.

Most ways and means exist on the furthest arc of extremes. On the one side is *suppression, violence, containment* and *eradication* representing the use of *control.* On the other side lies the *pacifism, suppression of feelings* and *submission* extremes. These are the *attack* or *worship* expressions the mind uses depending on its estimate of its self-worth ... in this case related to the degree to which it feels it has the power to *dominate* or be *crushed.* As with all mind dynamics neither extreme, or a less extreme combination of the two has *ever* resulted in genuine Peace.

Peace is never something you can *achieve* and *have* ... it is What You Are. The *'Peace that passes understanding'* means what the mind cannot comprehend because the mind deals always in opposites, comparisons and separation while the SELF is always ONE.

Balance is a natural expression of Peace and always find Its level just as does water. Peace is NOT something you can *work toward* or *get better at* or *become worthy of.* IT is a natural expression [facet] of Who You Really Are and is revealed to you as you *Ascend to* [become Aware of] the God You Are.

In the midst of chaos within the grand dream, You, standing in the Essence of the Peace You Are, effortlessly radiating that Peace and ALL can feel IT. Those in great resistance to Life will find you an enormous threat as has been illustrated throughout history [the illusion of time]. During long eons great Beings have been attacked, scourged and murdered in the name of Peace.

Others will feel the Peace You Are and be confused as chaos seems to dance with IT. A few will be deeply affected and be drawn to your Presence and turn inward to their own Peace [the same Peace – individuated].

You need DO nothing unless guided to. Peace will inform IT SELF whether to act or not.

Freedom

The Freedom fought for, longed for, voted for and sacrificed for is NOT Real Freedom. That Freedom is a body-mind-identity version that has many layers but never touches the *essence* of genuine Freedom.

One could live in a free country and yet be imprisoned in a thousand ways from incarceration to drug addiction to poverty. They could live in the same country in the lap of luxury and be tormented by guilt. They could have a loving family in a cozy corner of a beautiful little village and be a slave to their career.

Real Freedom exists everywhere all the time no matter the way the grand dream is playing out. It is an aspect of the Life you *are* where all attachments, expectations and identifications have been transformed and the world of time and space no longer molests you.

You could live in an environment where the liberty of the body-mind is severely restricted or even in a prison cell confined there for the rest of your physical experience, but this cannot touch the genuine Freedom You Are. This Awareness knows that Life cannot be restricted by the projected thoughts of conditioning because LIFE *is* Freedom IT SELF.

It does not *have* Freedom, which it could lose somehow like a country overcome by an outside oppressor. There are no oppressors in Life lived as ONE though a thousand dreams seek to confine and chain you. Only illusions can seem *contained and confined* beginning with the original bondage of believing you are no more than a tiny identity within a human form called *myself.*

The one who knows that they *are* Freedom IT SELF lives both IN a body-mind as well as limitlessly beyond any concept of identity. For example, for *some* who are Living as the Freedom they Are it is possible to experience Consciousness with an eagle flying over head or be ONE with a river or stream or mountain. Everything is Consciousness and when you know you are Freedom IT SELF the grand dream cannot confine you.

Abundance

At the very root of all conditioning is *shame, guilt, remorse* and *unworthiness.* Unworthiness is the first and most pervasive throughout the grand dream and as stated, began through the original *Descent of Consciousness* from the Awareness of the God You Are.

When You *as* God – ONE chose to *project* the playground of the universal dream with which to experience the Life You Are, you sank into *unconsciousness* of your True identity. As mentioned in PART ONE, the Garden of Eden allegory depicts God *expelling* [falling into a state of un-Consciousness of Who IT Really Is], ITs separated Consciousness from the Awareness *of* IT SELF. This expulsion triggered *unworthiness* and set in play the coloring of every aspect of the grand dream the sleeping God-SELF experiences.

It is the foundational reason that the manifesting of dreams through *Intention, Passion* and *Activity* often *fails* to reach fruition and it is the underlying reason that fully manifested dreams fail to bring with them the full experience of Abundance-Living.

Always the sleeper experiences fear of loss and anxiety concerning gain. Always the mind is in the rear-view mirror expecting disaster while clawing ever upward toward the hoped-for expectancy and security of *more*.

Living as the Abundance You Really Are is the full recognition that you are ALL THAT IS and can never lack anything that is Perfect for your experience in each Moment. This Awareness knows that Life has your back and will orchestrate every event perfectly, providing precisely what is required to fulfil every moment in total balance and Joy … whether IT uses an eye-dropper or an ocean to do so.

Beauty

The Beauty the false self observes can be truly exquisite. A glorious sunset, a pristine flower just as it opens, the innocent smile on a baby's face, a mist covered spider web, an inspiring piece of music, the wonder of a cloudless starry night, the panorama of the aurora borealis are just a few of numberless beautiful experiences the dreamer is exposed to.

To the degree that their conditioning [which veils the Truth], has been transformed, Beauty's essence is felt at deeper and deeper levels of Awareness. It is in the nature of Beauty to *break through* entrenched barriers and touch the coldest heart [conditioning] and for a moment expose Truth through the most resistant body-mind-identity to the imprisoned God-SELF.

It is not uncommon to witness one who is hardened to Life offering total devotion to a pet animal who offers the Beauty of unconditioned Love to its master. In this way the God-SELF shines through a chink in the armor of *control* that is smothering the Awareness of Truth.

However, when a false self is totally caught in the web of the grand dream, anger fear, rage and violent behavior are its reactions like a wretched, abused dog who has fended for itself under the most difficult circumstances, with anything that seems to threaten it met with extreme self-defensiveness. In this case even the *freeing* power of Beauty can be smothered.

Exquisite Music and Nature are two non-intrusive expressions of Beauty that usually do not stoke the fires of resistance in the most fearful false selves. In this way and others like them the SELF is able to reach ITs sleeping God-SELF without disturbing the waters of reactive emotion and touch IT with the *essence* of Truth.

When Beauty is fully experienced by the God-SELF, the sunset and the music are examples of *conduits* for this *essence* of Life that lies within. In Truth these conduits of Light exist *within* this essence, which is always ONE but *appears* outside it to the sleeping God-SELF. These sublime experiences can only be felt and NOT described since they are aspects of *infinity* which cannot be confined.

Joy

Happiness is partnered with *sorrow* and takes the false self on a roller coaster ride with every life experience. As stated before, the false self was originally made up out of the belief in separation from the original *Descent* of Consciousness from the Awareness of the ONE Life. From separation the belief in *opposites* manifested, from which all manner of conflict arose.

The entire universe is a projection on the screen of Consciousness *requiring the illusion of separation* in order to be available to the bodily senses, which then register as manifestations. There must be the *appearance* of a *here* and a *there* to simply cross the street, which itself must have the appearance of depth and width and length. In this way everything in the grand illusion *seems* to validate the reality of time and space.

We need this illusion in order to navigate within the dream of concepts and ideas, inspirations and visions. *It is not and was never a mistake* but part of the grand dream you as God-ONE used as your playground to know your SELF *through*.

The question is NOT *'is it real'* because it has a beginning and an ending and *'nothing that can be threatened exists'* [ACIM]. The question is, *'do you experience it consciously knowing it is un-real and thereby en-Joy it without being molested by it or are you un-consciously immersed in the quagmire of chaos and conflict separation offers to one who sleeps to Truth'*.

The answer is, we do both, enduring *'the slings and arrows of outrageous fortune'* [separation], eventually *transcending* the illusion [the *Ascent*] while remaining IN it … if you choose to.

When this occurs the happiness and sorrow *ride* … shifts into Joy, which is a *flat-line*, always present, even in the midst of the inevitable pain you experience while occupying a body. This is an unbroken state of *knowing* the illusion for what it is and allows that one to flow *through* the grand dream as the master *of* it.

It does not mean there is no interaction with the dream and that may include strong responses to the various ways the false self behaves. Jesus castigated the pharisees for their hypocrisy and scourged the money lenders for defiling the temple [a metaphor for the misuse of the Beauty that Life *is*]. The master [a conscious God-SELF] exemplifies Truth in every way ... Joy being a constant expression of IT. We are ALL masters and as such are always *in* Joy *as* Joy, but until we are Aware of this, very little of it stands out as the Truth of Who We Are.

Nevertheless, the deepest sleeper does experience vignettes of Joy ... also known as an *epiphany,* an *AHA* or a *momentary experience* of *Enlightenment.* Another example is when one is immersed in something they are totally *passionate* about. In these moments time often dissolves and that one is living in the NOW where the Joy You Are *is.*

When moved by the *Passion of Joy* you are expressing Truth in whatever way resonates with the moment, unaffected by any protest the dreaming world may offer. Joy is far more than a tranquil smile or the appearance of apparent bliss ... IT is the absolute *knowing* that *all is well, always,* no matter the outward appearance and that that state is Beauty, Love, Peace, Freedom, Abundance and Truth.

There are many other sub-headings that will become very visible as your path-less *Ascension* occurs. Here are a few … some, more than others will resonate with you as expressions of your unique God-SELF as it departs the long deep sleep and returns to full Conscious Awareness of the God-ONE IT *is.*

Compassion

The false self *pities* because it believes in *victims,* which is an expression of the belief in separation. Compassion is an expression of *un-condition-ed* Love that recognizes that the experience of *mental-emotional suffering* emanates from victim-hood.

It sees the God-SELF struggling with the paper chains of its own design but *does not fan the flames* of this illusion as does pity. It *comforts, lifts, serves* and *surrounds* this ignorance with its Awareness of Truth that the God-SELF has turned away from in its disguise as the false self and it is always available to those that reach within for the Real Life.

Humility

Arrogance is a shield hiding the deep-seated fear the false self lives within at some level in every moment. It is often completely invisible to the one who is expressing it, as it was for me for decades. I remember often being told by family, friends and business associates that I was arrogant, and I would instantly dismiss these comments as some kind of envy or delusion, giving it *no thought at all* because I was not *ready* to look within at my conditioning.

Humility recognizes that special-ness does not exist as there is only ONE and it is always Perfect. It knows that there *are no others* to compare to, only ONE cloaked and disguised in numberless versions of IT SELF in the playground of the grand dream.

The *fragrance* of humility is like a summer breeze wafting through a bed of roses that floods the Heart with Joy. It cannot be faked as the false self often attempts.

Spontaneity and Synchronicity

Spontaneity is the *essence* of *Being-in-the-flow of Life.* It requires total Trust that Life will *Live* you Perfectly in every moment. It says you *know* from deep in your Heart [God-SELF], not just intellectually that Life is unfolding perfectly no matter *how* it shows up.

It is an expression of this knowing that you are *not* in the way, *not* demanding, *not* trying to control or yearning for outcomes but see yourself [God-SELF] as an unattached Unicity ... in an ever-changing tapestry [within changeless-ness] of God expressing and experiencing IT SELF *as* You.

There is no courage required to Live this way because when you Live *as* this Conscious Awareness You Are, you are *fearless*, nothing *sticks* to you, you have no expectations and you are not trying to promote any identity that is dear to you.

A world of unexpected, fresh New Life shows up continuously and there is the natural Joyful and playful wonder that all new-born life experiences.

Everything is a *first* when you Live spontaneously where no baggage colors each moment. You pick up and discard effortlessly and always a ribbon of Gratitude wraps around each new experience. Nothing is missed that was meant for you and you are always in exactly the right place at the perfect moment … if only for a happy glance with another.

The tumblers to the vault of Love always fall into place as doors open everywhere for the Conscious God-SELF You Are to extend IT SELF to the world *of* IT SELF.

When you live Consciously *as* the God-SELF your Attention is NOT on the mundane activities and structures made up by the body-mind-identity in order to navigate its constantly shifting challenges born of the belief in separation. As a result, the Joy of simple things are never missed.

The step-by-step *blueprints* the false self uses each day as it moves through its version of Life often elude the God-SELF when it returns to full Conscious Awareness. And yet if something is required it will just show up and because you, as the individuated God-SELF are Now *listening* to the Silent Voice of Life … you will always be Aware of what IT is telling you.

This is how Life *orchestrates* your every experience effortlessly with everything from the seemingly most insignificant to the most earth-shaking events [as the false self sees them].

Spontaneity and Synchronicity is the way Life flawlessly provides you with each step and it is in the nature of Life to offer you *previews* of this simple way of living long before it becomes your every moment to moment experience. Everyone has experienced something like a parking spot showing up on a busy day just as they arrive at the store they were headed to.

They may have been telephoned seconds after thinking of someone or received money that dropped out of thin air just when they had run dry. Numberless serendipitous events occur every day for people around the world giving them a taste of Real Living that one day will become their norm.

Authenticity

Authenticity is a natural aspect of the God-SELF. It does not contain the compromises that *honesty* often contains ...

"Its just a little white lie."

... the false self will proclaim when referring to a judgment call it has made based on its unique conditioning and in an attempt to manipulate and control life into how it thinks it should play out. Even if the so-called motive is for the higher good there is always the odor of *self interest* in anything that emanates from the false self.

The integrity that is at the core of authenticity knows nothing of compromises. The SELF knows what is Perfect and sees far beyond the immediate circumstances to the entire Wholistic ONE-ness of All That Is. These words seem to suggest time and space, but the SELF sees both the moment and the entire tapestry of the ONE ... to IT, they are ONE. Looking simultaneously at a thread as well as infinity in the tapestry of Life does not add time and space to it. IT knows that to compromise the tiniest weave will ripple out into the entire experience with discord.

It is NOT possible for the false self to be authentic because it covets and protects its *special interests* based on its conditioning. The false self *does* compromise but its personal adjustments do NOT change the Perfection of All That Is … only its slanted perspective alters what cannot be tainted in essence. This is why for the false self there is one planet but almost 8 billion worlds, each one twisting and turning and writhing within their compromised expressions.

Transparency is an aspect of authenticity that hides nothing. When you are in the Presence of a Consciously Aware God-SELF you will always feel a *powerful essence*. You may very well feel uncomfortable since the Light of Truth reveals all that is imbalanced, but the heart of Peace always radiates from the Purity extended through transparency where there is never anything to hide … as *Truth castes no shadows.*

In this way the SELF will be the first to laugh *at* IT SELF since living in a body will bring with it the foibles of the grand dream. God's [Your] first expression is laughter and the Conscious God-SELF falls easily into the humor of tripping over its own shoe laces in whatever way.

Grieving

God grieves for God ... there *is* no other to grieve for. No matter what form IT occupies it is still God ... IT is still YOU. AS the false self, you become attached to forms and stories and when they depart you weep and feel loss and helplessness, the division between YOU and YOU *is* so convincing.

When you have made the upward turning *Ascent* toward full Conscious Awareness of Who You Really Are, there will be many episodes of grieving, not just for the loss of friends and family who no longer resonate with the frequency of Light that you are shifting into but especially for the loss of the *false identity* you have called yourself.

As your Awareness rises higher and higher you will also *allow* this sorrow to arise and be *felt* ... it lies deep within and has its origins in the first separation when the God You Are left ITs Awareness of IT SELF to hide within ITs many shells and dance the dance of forgetfulness. This loss was the first and deepest wound suggested in the Adam and Eve analogy. It was YOU that cast YOU out of the Garden of Conscious

Awareness ... the Awareness of the Heaven you Are through this *Un-Consciousness* of the God-SELF You Are.

From that original template the circle of *acquisition, possession* and *loss* continues to this day and the illusion of separation deepened the grief with each loss *believed in*. It must come up and be *felt* completely to arrive at the *root* of the illusion so that your Awareness of SELF, of the God You Are, can return.

Each loss is therefore a profound blessing and an opportunity *of your own making* to return the Light of Pure Conscious Awareness to you and with it the Freedom and the Peace That You Are.

Let Love Lead

Don't tell Love HOW IT's supposed to show up. It cannot be put in a cage like a prized captive bird whose song is beautiful but far from the infinite expression of Life it is when free to fly on its own. Unconditional Love is not just the expression of Who You Really Are ... it is also the open-ness to receive IT in whatever way it chooses to show up. Often, as you *open* to your God-SELF it will show up in ways the false self will resist and deny as having anything to do with its myopic view of Love.

It may show up as the loss of your dearest friend or mate, the destruction of a way of life, a heart attack … anything that opens your Heart at the exact place where it is most vulnerable. The loss of control, the agony of betrayal, the abandonment of a trusted friend are all signs of Love's all-encompassing Presence drawing you out of your rock-solid belief in the value of transient experiences.

It is not possible to lose Who You Are. You *can forget* this Truth for lifetimes, but the *essence of Truth* lingers and will seize every opportunity to remind you of the Beauty, the Freedom, the Joy that *is* You. *Let Love have its way* when it shows up. Be *vulnerable*, be *open*. Welcome it no matter how it appears. Always your highest purpose lies behind and within its appearances and if you do say *Yes* to its often fiery embrace it will remain with you, soon to outshine even the most pervasive dream of who you once believed you were … returning you to Freedom.

Being Nothing

I once taught A Course in Miracles for about 10 years then one day I read *again*, for maybe the 20th time a passage around page 1,000 that said: *"Forget this world. Forget this course and come with wholly empty hands unto your God"* [ACIM - W-pl.189.7:5]. Something *snapped* in me and I understood ... I really GOT IT! I have not read a spiritual book since ... and at this writing, that was about 14 years ago. I am not recommending this course of action, it was just the way I was guided, and it led me to what the same author said 2,000 year ago, [paraphrasing]: *"In the hour of your need it will be given to you."*

In many ancient texts we are told over and over again *'BE EMPTY', BE NOTHING', 'KNOW NOTHING'*. It's another way of saying, drop the person with all its acquired and memorized information and the myriad of interpretations that color and taint meanings that create numberless conflicts.

Being OPEN in each moment, EMPTY, KNOWING NOTHING means that you have died to person-hood, to personal identity and that is the greatest fear humanity has ... not physical death but *the death of identity*. Each one must finally reach this *line in the sand* where they become OPEN to Truth in *every* moment from an Unknown, Unseen Source letting the fickle and unreliable influence of a *personal identity* go.

Suffering is *the great persuader* that draws most people to that *line* where the great *"AHA – I GOT IT"* can dawn upon their Consciousness. This usually occurs when they are on their knees where suffering has put them. It is there that they *finally* make the *choice* to BE NOTHING.

The Body, Suffering and Residual Karma

As mentioned, suffering is a direct response to the belief in victims, which in turn emanates from a belief in separation. This made-up response is directly tied to the mind's thoughts and emotions and when you shift from *mind-thought* to *Heart-Feelings* [the awakened God-SELF's way of communicating], mental and emotional suffering dissolves.

However, while Consciousness occupies a body, pain is inescapable. Body pain can be chronic even after you have shifted from *Awakening* to *Ascension* where Attention is firmly focused on Who You Really Are. The residual momentum of karma generated while your Attention was pointed directly into the grand dream will still be showing up even though you are stepping off that wheel into the Silence of nothing-ness.

It is not uncommon to witness a master Being walking with a crutch or leaving the body due to cancer and while that one still occupied a body, physical pain and suffering *was* present. This is also a Divine Dichotomy but that *physical suffering does not suggest* the error of a separated Consciousness.

Further, when you are making the shift totally into the full Conscious Awareness of the God You Are, this *physical suffering* is endured with *compassion* for yourself as well as all who suffer unconscious of Truth. While it certainly is possible to still experience grumpy and irritating moments, there is *never any guilt or shame* associated with these expressions ... you are simply expressing your God-human-ness.

The NOW

NOW Consciousness is not about *clock time*, not about some small fraction of a second that can still be measured as an aspect of time and space. It is *God Awareness*, Awareness of the God-SELF you Are. All experiences in this Awareness are timeless and can therefore NOT take on any additional karmic influences.

Since this Awareness is not of time and space where the illusion of separation seems to exist, the Awareness of the ONE Consciousness or I AM is an ever-present experience ... it *is* Reality. This is also known as *Stillness* or *Silence* and can occur in the midst of deep Silence or in the roaring thunder of a big city where the *noise* of distraction is everywhere. It is literally *the eye of this storm* which swirls around and through the false self's moment to moment experience.

This is genuine Peace, the Peace You Are ... not *have*, but *are*. It far transcends any concept of *peace of mind*, which at best is a transient experience that usually has many *not-so-peaceful thoughts* going on beneath its shallow radar that has very little Awareness of *anything*, not the least of which is the programmed conditioning that is functioning like a computer behind the scenes as it orchestrates the myopic world of the body-mind-identity's world.

Chapter Four

SELF DISCOVERY
THE PATHLESS PATH HOME

The Old Ways

Any concept that involves time and space to somehow lead you HOME to Freedom or Truth or Self Realization [there are many terms], is *a delay tactic* since Truth is only ever and always NOW. You *are* HOME Now and simply have your Attention turned toward the grand dream, which keeps it alive *in* and *as* your experience.

However, this dream has been your life experience for so long that it is *very difficult* for the imprisoned God-SELF to believe that the grand dream is NOT real, and that returning HOME is simple. It is far easier to accept that this beautiful *alternative* to the life IT knows so well *might* be achieved *through really serious effort and time* ... perhaps over many lifetimes depending on what belief system IT is exposed to.

As a result, in the energy of time and space, those who were already HOME created systems to accommodate this belief since very few would accept that HOME could be experienced in an instant. These systems include a wide variety of disciplines, practices and modalities combined with a variety of time oriented prophetic ways and means to provide a kind of bird's eye view of what might be coming.

Crystal gazing, palm reading, astrology, reading tea leaves, the I Ching, tarot cards, channeling and many other concepts offered insights into how things *might be going*. Even those who are totally immersed in the grand dream and have no interest at all in returning HOME [if they even believe in such a thing] have visited so called fortune tellers and may even read their daily horoscope forecast in the local newspaper.

All concepts that place Freedom *out in the future* where it does NOT exist, are part of the grand dream themselves and as such not one of these systems or concepts has ever brought one HOME … but they have had and still have a significant influence on those who adhere to them and eventually *do* bring them to *the threshold* where Self Discovery [Self Inquiry], *not a time oriented path,* is approached. This usually comes as a result of exhaustion and frustration as it did for me where nothing had brought more than a vignette of the Real Life [as beautiful as they may have been].

Self Discovery

Self Discovery is simple. It means,

'Standing in the fire of who you are NOT so that Who you Really Are can be revealed'

It's like clearing the clouds that hide the sun that *has always been there.* This begins through the Mirrors of your unique World.

These mirrors *trigger* you through stories and dramas - the conditioning that defines your false self , which is *ready* to be transformed.

The transformation is accomplished by *GRACE* [Love in Action] after you have slipped beneath the stories and dramas and into the *FEELINGS* that cause these events and *Felt* them fully. Once you have *EMBRACED* these *feelings* [since they too are aspects of All That IS] ... Grace steps in.

Self Discovery requires that you are ready to make the *NO MATTER WHAT* choice to be FREE. Without that choice, as with the time-oriented systems ... HOME will remain a hoped-for aspect of the grand dream that at best will deliver beautiful vignettes of the Real Life.

In Self Discovery we are not speaking about *emotions* which are the instruments of the mind. What occurs in the FEELING nature is to go beneath the story/drama where the conditioning resides ... it is generic, as said its roots being *guilt, shame, remorse and unworthiness* and branching out from there.

This is like using a laser beam instead of a shotgun to target what lies behind the manifestations that occur in stories/dramas and eliminates the need to analyse, which is an endless process like a dog-mind chasing its tail.

SELF DISCOVERY
Story/Drama

Triggers
False self 'Reacts'

God-SELF 'Responds'
By recognizing experiences as

Pointers
To Conditioning that is ready to be
Transformed

There, God-SELF is
Neutral/Objective

God-SELF 'FEELS'
Beneath the story/dramas

Then 'EMBRACES' these Feelings

'GRACE' – Love in Action
Transforms Conditioning

The Mechanics

The pathless-path is always the same with any story/drama/mirror-trigger bringing Attention to conditioning.

The mirrors are meant to get your Attention. You are triggered *on* the grand dream's stage *as* the false self and there you are looking at the story/drama trigger *subjectively* with all the emotions and attitudes associated with the false self as it exists at the moment.

When you recognize a mirror as a trigger you step *off* the stage and look at the trigger *objectively* without your connection to the false self or any judgments that may be sticking to it. In this way *you* are neutral and this allows the SELF to speak to the awakening God-SELF.

Here is where it is possible to FEEL the conditioning *without* the story/drama. For example, what does *envy* FEEL like without a story, or *resentment, victim-hood* and many, many other feelings? You [the Awakening God-SELF - *YOU*] is simply FEELING these feelings without trying to *fix* or *change* them until the feelings *subside*. Then *YOU* EMBRACE these feelings and GRACE transforms that *layer* of conditioning.

EMBRACING in this case is both a sign of *Gratitude* for receiving the trigger as well as genuine *SELF Love,* which is *Love* of the God-SELF ... *Love of God. This* Love is *the instrument* of power that dissolves or transforms illusions.

Turning Over Every Stone

When you choose Freedom NO MATTER WHAT, it means *turning over every stone* that hides the conditioning that defines your false self and keeps it alive to continue molesting you and hiding the sleeping individuated God-SELF from IT SELF. This is not literal, you are *not seeking* ... *"what about this or that* ... or, *is there something in there I need to look at and figure out?"* ... as the false self would attempt to do.

The *mirrors* in your world are the instruments the fully Conscious SELF uses to trigger your *Attention* to what is ready to be *transformed.* They will show you without you *searching* and without *effort* on your part.

An insult that wounds you, a reckless driver that cuts you off yelling at you while they rush by bringing up anger and rage, a television show that highlights the life of the rich and famous that instills envy, a news bulletin that profiles the trafficking of children and imparts contempt or even a sense of helplessness to somehow influence or stop these kinds of atrocities from happening.

These are mirror-triggers that surround your life experiences showing you what to look at. If you continue to look at these triggers *subjectively* you are judging *out there* and are very much *involved in* the miasma of the events. When you step off the stage you become *objective* and are then able to *disconnect* from the story.

In that Conscious environment it is possible to slip beneath the stories/dramas and into the *feelings* that caught your Attention through the mirror. Then you will recognize the cause of the conditioning that is ready to be transformed. From the root system of *guilt, shame, remorse* and *unworthiness* branches will show up that are specific to each triggered feeling. Hopelessness for example is associated with unworthiness,

"Who am I to think I could make any significant change that will help others or the world or even myself? Poor me!"

Remember, none of this is True but it certainly *feels* True and must be *felt fully* otherwise it returns to the cauldron of conditioning to simmer beneath the surface of Conscious Awareness producing more and more dysfunctional experiences that resonate with it.

You don't try to *get-rid-of* of these feelings ... you simply *Feel* them and when the fire subsides you *Embrace* the feelings no matter how disgusting they may have been. This is genuine *SELF Love* because the SELF-GOD-ONE is *All That Is* ... excluding nothing. The so-called positive and negative that don't exist in Truth, are aspects of an infinite scale that is an endless spiral within ONE-ness.

Everything is an aspect of Pure Conscious Awareness. The mind cannot grasp the concept of the absence of positive and negative because its existence lives within the illusion of opposites borne of the belief in separation. There is no need to understand this, simply accept the *Unknowable* Truth *with your Embrace.* Love in

Action or Grace can then transform this aspect of conditioning back into the nothing-ness from which it arose.

Actually, nothing has really happened ... the Conscious Awareness of Who You Really Are has simply been lifted *[Ascended]* a little more out of the prison that has held it captive for eons. This is the lightning fast pathless-path HOME.

Chapter Five

THE MIRRORS OF LIFE

As you live deeper in the Heart,

the mirror gets clearer and clearer
- Rumi

The infinite projections that took Pure Conscious Awareness on the spiral of *Descent* into the loss of Awareness of Who You Really Are, *are* also the instruments for bringing about the *Ascent* of Conscious Awareness by reflecting *back to you* who you are *NOT* ... the conditioning that has made up the false-self-body-mind-identity you have believed is you.

In Truth, it always reflected back to you who you are NOT, but in the beginning, you were totally immersed in *the grand dream of separation* and the *victim-hood belief* that was created by that belief. As a result, you were very busy *placing blame* for everything nasty that befell you on *them* or *God.*

It was always the conditioning that *veiled* the Truth of Who You Are, and the transformation of that conditioning is like dispersing clouds that reveals the sun that was *always* present.

Relationship Mirrors

When your consciousness is deep asleep in the grand dream of separation *everything* seems as if it is *out there* and is looked upon as either friend or foe ... usually a combination of both.

Depending on the degree to which *you judge* these separate entities and circumstances, you either *attack* or *worship* them. This too is usually a combination of both although this amalgam of reactions is often hidden beneath deeper and deeper belief systems that are intertwined with your conditioning.

The most pervasive of these are relationships, not just the partnerships with other individuals such as a mate or spouse but also the many other forms of relationship the deep sleeper forms. These include the work environment, the government [yours and others], the religious or spiritual concepts you may relate to, fashion trends, philosophies and a host of more subtle relationships such as the cars you drive, the computing systems you use, the television programs and movie genres you follow. There are endless relationships that captivate, distract, engage and seem to validate the existence of the false self you call *yourself.*

What makes these mirrors so powerful in triggering the awareness of conditioning is the *consistent presence* of them offering endless opportunities to shift from *out there* comparisons, judgements and analysis to *inside feelings.* This is why it is *not uncommon* for relationships to end when you have moved *inside* and as a result begun to *expand awareness* while the other partner or relationship environment has not.

Intensely Painful Mirrors

Consciousness is *always* leading IT SELF back to the full Awareness of Who It Really Is. It [the sleeping God-SELF] has been buried under the influence of separation for countless eons and the illusion of individuality is so fixed in place that each expression of it has a hard shell around this True Being.

To break through this thick shield, to create a chink in its ancient protective armor the SELF uses whatever is effective in the moment. Intense heart-rending events are often employed as one of those break-through influences. The loss of a beloved child, spouse or friend can rip holes in any heart that is shrouded in self defensive walls.

For example, the phenomena of beached whales may draw tears and induce an ache to the heart, which is sign of the SELF being *Freed*. Child abuse and human trafficking can bring up intense anger and rage but also again, rip away at the threads that bind the individuated sleeping God-SELF.

Consciousness *does not plan* these things ... *IT doesn't plan anything* at all, which would require the use of time, space and agendas ... and therefore separation. IT uses the dysfunction caused by conditioning to awaken IT SELF. IT uses the dream to wake IT SELF *from* the dream, and the entire dream *is* dysfunctional.

"There is an ancient wakefulness that will eventually 'startle' us back to the Truth of Who We [Really] Are."
- Rumi

Nothing is wasted, Consciousness uses everything to direct your Attention *inward* toward the Love, the Truth, the Light IT *is*. The false self has its own judgmental interpretations, but it is incapable of recognizing Truth or genuine unconditioned Love. The Heart [sleeping God-SELF] can *feel* the tender fragrance and essence of Love that lingers around the most heart-wrenching events and this is what helps to nudge it [often powerfully] out of ITs ancient sleep.

Of course, the false self can and has used such events to amplify its closed and defensive nature laden with fear as it is, and this can … for a long while, take it deeper into the *denial* of the Truth it has been exposed to through these intensely painful mirrors. However, each event like this is a seed … some germinating over many lifetimes and others growing much sooner … nothing of Truth is ever lost, being an aspect of eternity.

Embrace it all. Allow the grief to come up and feel it all until the Grace You Are transforms the events back into the Pure Light that is behind every projection on the screen of Consciousness. All the while, say YES to What Is, NO MATTER WHAT and the ancient *and* recent seeds will reveal their secrets, always leading you HOME in some way.

Perfect Mirrors

You can only *ever* be in environments that resonate with *who* you believe you are. Every such setting *is* a Perfect mirror. Everything from the most dramatic panorama to the tiniest subtle experience is a *precise mirror* for this belief.

If you go to work the same way every day and one day change that route for no apparent reason, that slight alteration somehow mirrors an aspect of your unique conditioning-frequency.

Judging Mirrors

When you catch yourself judging conditioning that somehow disturbs you, be aware that this is *always* the false self judging itself. Its reaction may exhibit repulsion and immediately it may *resolve* to do better by trying to *fix* that conduct. But there is no fix because nothing Real is happening. *YOU have never done anything wrong* nor are you capable of it.

It is common to hear the false self speak about being *this or that*. The SELF, which is ONE appearing as many has no *add-ons*. It does not have a *personality*. It does not have *peculiarities, peccadilloes or foibles* ... nothing *sticks* to it. It *cannot be offended* because it has no special traits that can be criticized. It *cannot offend* because it always speaks only to the SELF *in* and *as* anyone it addresses. It cannot feel *a sense of loss* because it is NOT attached to anything even though the host body-mind-identity may be extremely wealthy and prominent. It *has* no *identity* of any kind because it is *empty*. It *knows nothing* because it does not accumulate historical knowledge ... *it knows what it needs to know in the moment of ITs need.*

The false self's belief in its reality *as* the real you is so pervasive that it really thinks it is trying to somehow get better and qualify for Freedom ... the very Freedom it would quickly withdraw from if it ever got close.

Always the answer is to *Respond* to the mirror/triggers pointing to the conditioning that is ready to be transformed, *Feel* them fully, *Embrace* them and *Grace* will then *Transform* each layer of conditioning that has arisen.

Feeling

Feeling is an instrument used by the SELF to expose the deeply buried conditioning that *hides* or *veils* the Truth of Who You Truly Are.

Feelings are not to be confused with *emotions* when for example someone says: *"I don't want to hurt your feelings."* The SELF cannot be hurt, insulted/offended, manipulated or influenced in any way by the false self because IT *has* no conditioning attached to it to defend.

When you are experiencing something that *triggers* you such as the sudden departure of a partner, the false self will go through many expressions of emotion. Depending on how frustrated and as a result *open* you are with the drama/dream of life, your sleeping God-SELF will *emerge* and FEEL *beneath* the emotions finding the ancient conditioning that is the real *cause* of all the stories/dramas.

In this case deep seated *feelings* of *abandonment* and *betrayal* may come up. *Anger, rage* and *hatred* may be followed by deep *sorrow, hopelessness* and *helplessness* ... all *disconnected* completely from the current *story* that *triggered* these *feelings*.

Feelings and Intuition

The bondage of the body-mind-identity has been long and deep but never so imprisoned as with the *educated mind* that believes Truth can be discovered through thought and analysis. All philosophy falls under this *spell*, filled with ideas, concepts, perspectives, conjecture and complicated explanations. Truth is *revealed* through your *Feeling Nature*. Feelings *know*, while thoughts and emotions have a wide range of descriptions colored by one's own individual and unique conditioning.

The Feeling Nature *is* your *Intuition*, which cannot be *thought* into being where it will show you ITs revelations. IT simply speaks spontaneously in the moment and provides *full blown visions* that are like Light shining through the infinite facets of the diamond of Truth. The Intuition cannot be *learned* … it simply IS and instantly connects [yet without distance or time] to All Knowledge.

IT is NOT something you *develop* through spiritual practices … nothing that is Real can be *improved* – only *discovered* as an ever-present aspect of Who You Really Are. Truth is always about *discovery*, not *development* since Truth has *never NOT been* … and you *are* Truth. The simplest way-less way is to remove [transform] what is NOT Truth [so that IT may shine fully throughout your Conscious Awareness]. This is *Self Discovery*, the most direct route on your *Ascent* Home to the full Awareness of the God You Are.

Nothing Really Matters

When you attend a movie that *moves* you in some way, regardless of its theme or tone, it sticks with you *for a while* after leaving the theater and may even touch various sensitive aspects of your current life experience. But ultimately, you know it was *just* a movie, not real and does NOT matter in the big scheme of what most call reality.

This applies *exactly* the same to the grand dream that most of humanity is living in and believes is real … *it doesn't really matter simply because it's is NOT real.* To the false self this is highly offensive since it takes so much of its life experiences so *seriously* and treats much of it as sacred … to be revered and respected.

The SELF You Are however, *cannot offend nor can it be offended* because, as stated already, nothing sticks to IT. Nor does IT speak *to* the false self or body-mind-identity, which IT knows cannot comprehend anything it offers. IT is *always* speaking to the sleeping God-SELF Who is IT SELF presently imprisoned.

The only value of the grand dream while you sleep, is as an environment where the imprisoned God-SELF can find ITs way HOME, usually initially through pain and suffering.

There is nothing about the life of anyone that dances in the grand dream that is of *any real value* whatsoever, only insofar as it directs your Attention *inward* where Truth resides. All the monuments and statues and plaques and memorials are aggrandizements to the body-mind-identity's false image … even the great heroes throughout history serve no one except to the extent that Attention is *shifted inward* toward Truth.

When you make the NO MATTER WHAT choice to be FREE you must become *ruthless* with the multitude of distractions the false self utilizes to keep you distracted and always ask, *'Is this of Truth?"* ... then the SELF will show you, with absolute certainty what benefits your *pathless-path* HOME.

Silence or Stillness

Silence or *Stillness* is often referred to in various spiritual teachings as the single most important thing required to bring you HOME to Truth. The false self or body-mind-identity cannot bear its own Silence and needs to be perpetually involved in something, not just the cacophony of the grand dream but also in the endless ways and means contained in the myriad of spiritual modalities available, which are the avenues it uses to distract the now *Ascending* God-SELF from the heart of *Silence.*

Silence or Stillness ... that *is* Peace, *is not the absence of noise*, it **is *emptiness* ... *the absence of person-hood.*** When Peace becomes a *conscious choice,* you begin to experience *Emptiness-Peace* frequently, which, if it becomes your primary focus unfolds into your only Reality.

If you *do* choose Peace [by any name] *Emptiness must follow* because the Peace You Are *is* empty, meaning devoid of the friction caused through the conditioned and fragmented mind that believes it is a separate individual. This is the simplicity of Freedom and requires no complicated gymnastics involving long and arduous practices.

Freedom or Peace or Self Realization is simply a choice which when given undivided Attention [with *no* mind-oriented definitions added] *finds its own way* within the labyrinth of your conditioning. Your only job [so called] is to maintain your Attention on Peace.

> *Silence isn't the absence of sound,*
> *its the absence of self.*
> *- Anthony De Mello*

Follow The Wound

In times of escalating confusion, chaos and conflict one can feel severely attacked, insulted, offended, deflated, manipulated, discouraged, helpless, hopeless and in general – *wounded*.

It may be difficult to accept that *everything experienced* that seems to wound *is* a reflection of *your own conditioning* mirrored back to you for your highest good. When you are in the *thick of it*, it feels so much easier to *point the finger* at perpetrators *out there* who seem to be the *cause* of your discomfort.

They *are* the catalysts and conduits for discovering who you are NOT and if you will *follow the wound* deep down inside your *Feelings*, leaving the story that triggered them behind, you *will* discover the ancient conditioning that manifests your sorrow in the world you experience. It's a *crumb trail* created by your SELF to help you *remove the rubble* from the earth-quake of your dream-life so that IT/You may return to the Throne of Power as the fully Awakened God-SELF You Are.

When your God-SELF *is* Free, your world [which is still a dream that you then are *fully* Awake in] will show up far differently. It will reflect the Peace you have always dreamt of and manifest effortlessly without planning, agendas or world changes of any kind. When what used to cause you discord does show up, as it surely will within the dream, *compassion* will have replaced judgment ... again without effort.

Real Life is Light

> *Life lived Truly is light, joyful,*
> *playful and never serious.*

It is very common to see spiritually oriented people acting and speaking *very seriously*, *sternly* and even *strictly*. This is like a tightly clenched fist that nothing cannot enter. The body is the first evidence of this through scowl and anger lines on the face, stiff limbs and illnesses related to tightness such as heart disease, breathing disorders, constipation, stiff muscles and many others.

When you are living *as* the Freedom You Are it is normal to be child-like, often giddy, laughing at the play of life and over-joyed with the simple things that children hold in awe and wonder.

When the Heart is Open [Awareness is Expanding] these kinds of *Freedom* symptoms appear spontaneously and are *never contrived* or *thought* into existence.

Life Lives You

As stated repeatedly, it is NOT possible to offend or belittle the SELF who has no need of approval in any way since IT knows IT is All That Is and therefore totally *complete*. IT knows IT is Truth. IT knows IT SELF as ONE, lacking nothing and *this* is Who You Are. This is what Life *is*.

When one becomes Aware of this, which at first will only be *an intellectual concept*, the most direct route HOME is to allow *Life to Live You* since IT knows the direct pathless-path out of the dark forest of delusions that have bound your Sleeping Beauty God-SELF for eons.

The way to do this is to say YES to *What Is* in every moment. This does NOT mean agreeing with everything that is occurring in your life. If you find yourself in a position where you can intervene in some way where for instance where some form of abuse is happening ... *then you are there for a reason*. But when that is done, shake off the experience, not attaching yourself to it in any way such as joining a new *cause,* unless ... in some way, the Joy of such an activity *temporarily* resonates with you.

You are saying YES to What Is because it *is* happening, and this is *non-resistance*, but you are NOT agreeing with that particular event. In this way you are able to Love the SELF that is temporarily playing the parts of victim and perpetrator without endorsing the actors' behavior. This is the meaning of *Living IN the world but not OF the world.*

When you have made the NO MATTER WHAT choice to return to the full Conscious Awareness of Who You Really Are … [God – SELF – I AM – Life], it seems like all of Heaven joins in supporting your quest. Heaven *is* this Conscious Awareness, *NOT a location*, which would place IT in time and space and therefore separation.

It *is* this Consciousness that metaphorically takes two steps toward you for every one of yours. This *is* the prodigal son allegory, *"For this son of mine was dead and is alive again! He was lost and is found"*. *You know* that you are both the Father and the Son … the ONE SELF as well as the God-SELF individuated.

In this deep *surrender* of the *dream-free-will* to the God-WILL, Life takes over as the captain of your experience. Life *is* the SELF, *is* the God

You Are and knows each Perfect step on the pathless-path HOME. This NO MATTER WHAT choice *informs* Life that you [the quickly *Ascending* sleeping God-SELF] will follow *only* Truth and ITs *every suggestion* no matter where it leads you.

This guidance will *brighten the mirrors* of your world, triggering again and again the conditioning that is ready to be transformed. It will come in waves and like tsunamis, they will often overwhelm the false self's *now tenuous hold* over your [sleeping God-SELF's] Freedom, the Freedom You Are.

This phase is not for the faint-hearted toe-dipper who still craves a comfortable pew at the feet of glory. It is a *fiery phase* where everything you are NOT is *burned away*. This fire will come over and over as a *fiercely-gentle* lover.

These great gifts often come wrapped in disguise and often, if not usually at first are not recognized as the profound blessings they are. Finding your SELF through loss is a common example.

So many veils shroud the Light and *you have become accustomed to living in shadows declaring it to be Light* when all it is, is a dim reflection of the True Brilliance You Are. This way is strewn with the bodies of conditioned sacred beliefs and hallowed possessions.

There *will* be moments to breath and rest and then another wave, which can come in any way that is Perfect to place you firmly in front of the lies that have shackled you to littleness and limitation. But you will become increasingly Aware that you are always *surrounded by enormous loving help* and *deep gratitude* will be your constant companion.

For me, just on the physical level, it was one who had already crossed the bridge … a fiery Kali that was relentless as she led me through *the valley of the shadow of death* over and over again. The height of her volcanic passion was matched only by the depth of her unconditional Love. Had I not recognized this Love as Real, I would have run many times, which was my *chosen escape* when *the going got tough* throughout the sleeping life I had led before.

Life gives you exactly what you require to make it through the *mind-field* of *conditioning-transformation* and IT cannot be fooled *["God is not mocked"*] ... IT knows when you are Truly ready. The Awareness of Truth beyond the last battleground with the false self is indescribable, which is always the case since *infinity cannot be framed.*

I write and speak *around* Truth, pointing *to* what IT is NOT, but the inner court is veiled and can only be *felt* by each one. Remaining in a physical body after that is an effortless Joy where *none of the dream sticks* and each moment undresses before your grateful gaze blessing you and all Life, usually without your Awareness of the Light that is left behind in your wake. This is the True Life that is available to you Now if you so choose.

Truth is Simple
and as Life Living You,
does all the heavy lifting without assistance
Belief, Faith, Trust and Knowing

The false self holds a host of *beliefs* that act as its safety net when walking the tightrope of a life it considers shaky at best. Its beliefs give it a sense of continuity and allows it to feel embraced to some extent by *known* things. Others have the same beliefs, and this gives it the added feeling of security based on safety in numbers.

Faith is the active participation in *beliefs* and is expressed well beyond religious concepts into the business world, social settings, behavior and virtually anything that requires consistency, again giving the false self the feeling that it can rely on its *beliefs* to perform the same every time it calls on them to help it navigate through the dangerous waters of its daily existence ... as it sees it.

Trust goes beyond *faith* and approaches *surrender* in its essence. It says that the false self is beginning to let go of *its need for control* and is part of the experience of *Living Lightly* that occurs as the God-SELF Awareness is expanding beyond simple *Awakening*. Nevertheless, if Trust is placed in *transient things,* results will always be illusionary.

Knowing lacks any *doubt*, which is still present in *beliefs, faith* and *trust*. The God-SELF lives always in an unbroken state of *Unknowing*, which is where *Knowing* arises when there is a need for it. *IT literally Knows that NOT knowing is the conduit to Knowing. Emptiness is Peace.* It is *quiet, still* and *silent* even in the midst of chaos and conflict because there are no attachments of any kind. Then, when something needs to be Known or done ... Knowing simply shows up. *This is the Freedom You Are.*

The Sleeping World

The I AM Presence is any version of the God You Are such as *Freedom* or *Love* that happens to prevail at the moment. Its like looking out from the inside of a Pure crystal through windows [facets] that have different *energy signatures.*

As the I AM Presence expands in your Awareness you will witness the world and its occupants more and more as sleeping. This sleep is an *essence* like a hypnotic state that you are now able to easily recognize. Everything that once seemed so important will now seem insignificant. You will laugh at how *serious* you once took the world to be.

This Awakened state is NOT the same as the mind-oriented AHA that awakens you to the Awareness that the world you have been living in is NOT real. It is the actual *unbroken experience* of *witnessing the grand dream 'as' a dream.* No words can describe this unmistakable and consistent feeling that never again leaves your Awareness. This occurs when within the *Ascent* HOME, *Life is Truly Living You.*

Freedom In The Great Dream

Nothing in the great dream is Real except *that which does not come and go.* The simple Awareness of this can *instantly* defuse all mental and emotional suffering. It can dissolve all worry about a dream future and all remorse about a dream past. It can halt all judgment and bring fear to a standstill. It can leave you Silent, open and available, transforming the conditioning that defines the false self into nothing-ness ... your True state.

Take away the musical chairs that come and go and what is left ... just YOU ... *Pure Conscious Awareness,* which may also be called Joy, *Truth, Freedom, Abundance, Peace, Beauty Love* [now unconditioned], the fully Conscious God-SELF - I AM.

These expressions of Consciousness have no beginning or ending. They are *unborn* Reality.

You Are this Reality and even *if* you linger *in* the dream, for whatever reason, it cannot molest this Real YOU … the Consciously Aware God-SELF.

It is your playground and now the Love You Are swells compassionately for all who still sleep within the grand dream. You are Aware of their suffering but Know that you must allow each aspect of the ONE Consciousness to return to the Freedom IT is, on ITs own. You do not interfere but are available when the moment arrives, if it arises to *point* to what is NOT Truth.

You speak, or you are Silent as the moment requires and *hold nothing as sacred* except the Truth residing in all Life. The chaos and frantic activity within the great dream swirls around you and yet you are unmoved unless called to shed a moment's Light here or there … perhaps in words or comfort or encouragement but then you move on, never attached to anything which comes and goes.

The Being that is Aware of IT SELF is *Truly the Light of the world* and this, without the need of a word or any activity. All Life bends toward the grandeur of this Light like a garden of flowers to the day's sun. No explanation is required for the flower to respond to the sunlight, it simply knows *'this is Life'*.

There is a powerful gentleness, an indescribable influence flowing through the Stillness of Truth that even the deepest sleeper can sense, although to them it registers as a disturbance to their entrenched beliefs with the possible reaction of deep resistance or even attack. Freedom does not react to this but simply resides in tranquility unless called upon to rebuke the ignorance.

Each moment is unique and has no forebear to influence it, no hoped-for outcome to sway each pristine untouched expression. Your *constant example* is radiant and gentle. None of this is contrived ... it just IS.

No Struggle

The Freedom You Are is *revealed* ... NOT *earned* or *struggled-for* through great effort. It appears naturally and gently when the illusion that seems to hide it has dissolved. That illusion requires *Life Force* to exist, without it, like everything in the grand dream ... it fades back into nothing-ness.

As said often, it is made up of *conditioning,* which has what looks like numberless masks but without your *Attention,* the Life Force that animates it is gone and it dissolves.

-Recognizing the **Mirrors** *your unique world shows you*

-and the **Triggers** *that emanate from them,*

-then **Feeling** *and* **Embracing** *them*

-so that **Grace** *can* **Transform** *them*

-is the most **direct route** *to the* **Freedom** *that You Are*

But … for those whose Passion cannot be tamed and *must* **BE Free Now** *…****within this direct route****,* simply *withdrawing* your *Attention* from ***everything except Freedom****, WILL* return to you the Conscious Awareness of Who You Really Are.

Your Focused Attention on Freedom [or I AM, or Love, or Peace or Beauty or Abundance or Joy]

-is a ***DECLARATION*** of Truth

-existing *Now as* You

-and that is where Life Force then flows

-*EXPANDING* it

-*until there is nothing else*

It's like an express Train to Heaven.

Chapter Six

THE CHANGING DREAM - *ASCENT*

The one who has chosen Freedom NO MATTER WHAT is focused *intently* on Who They Really Are. They have Awakened from the long deep sleep of forgetfulness as the God They Are and know on some level [at first intellectually] that this *is* the Truth. Whatever label they use to describe this Truth may vary widely but always it means the same thing.

Returning HOME to this Conscious Awareness is *experiential* and leaves the *mind-idea* of Freedom or Truth behind in the world of dreams. **It is NOT really an *Ascent* but an *Awareness* of What Is and has always been.**

For most who choose this pathless-path nothing else distracts them and they are often alone, and seldom seen involved in spiritual group gatherings, movements or causes. They *know* that the greatest service they can render is to BE fully Conscious of Who They Really Are as this

Light radiates out to the entire world and influences *so called change* far more than all the causes combined.

This change is NOT *of* the grand dream that so many promote, but of the *focused Attention* that the *Awakened* choose, which directs them more and more *inward*. In this way when they experience the dream world, they experience God *in* and *as* everything ... despite appearances.

While there are many examples of *change-oriented achievements* by great ones who have returned fully to the Conscious Awareness of Who They Really Are, the only *Real change* their so-called work achieved was *to influence the turning of Attention inward* where HOME resides through what most would call – *Touching the Heart.*

*When full Conscious Awareness is restored, 'identification' with Consciousness can **still** be an 'attachment' ... and YOU are **before** Consciousness.*

At this point the I AM Presence

will take you to the

UNKNOWABLE

*which has no **name** or **form***

LOVE IS WHO

YOU ARE

Love tears away the hardened threads of pride

Bringing the arrogance of ages to its knees

It begs of no one but is never empty

Love smiles gently in the face of hatred

And embraces those that defile Its name

*Never judging, knowing that IT lies beneath the
most stubborn resistance*

*The Angels of Peace wrap their wings around
the unloved*

Flying on the breath of Life

Reminding the sorrowed Heart that it is always Loved

Never was there a moment when you were not Loved

Never was a dark mind without the Light of Love

Its brilliance shines at the slightest opportunity

You are never without Love

No matter how deep you have fallen

For Love is Who you Are

Mind hears only lofty words

But the Heart – your True Self

FEELS the Truth of this

About the Author

John McIntosh

A Multi-millionaire until 1999 John traveled for decades speaking to tens of thousands of people before leaving everything behind and diving into Self-Discovery. John shares his acquired understanding of the ancient energy of the *mind* together with his personal experience of the Now Energy - ***Thinking with the Heart***, which is the instrument of Self Discovery, the direct route HOME to Truth.

John's website: http://johnmcintosh.info

[where you will find all John's books]

Testimonials

I'm reading a book by John and have discovered he is the most profound writer I've come across in many years. - Deanna Lockhart

I just wanted to express my gratitude for your writing. Thank you so much for living in Truth and effortlessly sharing it. - Сла Ва

In gratitude to you for helping me come Home to myself. - Anu Mahal

You express with such clarity and simplicity through your ability to communicate the Truth. The words serve as pointers, but the revelation is beyond the words, transcending them. Eternal gratitude dear John. - Christine Van Hoose

Your wisdom has been the sacred oil in my lamp, the grace-filled grease on my wheel of samsara, turning the phantoms of fear into knowing, the illusions into inspiration, the chaos into coherence. I am deeply grateful for the pearls, the keys, the doors you have opened in my heart and mind. All with infinite Love and patience. I am grateful. - Pamela Jane Gerrand

MAY THE LIGHT

OF TRUTH

THAT YOU ARE

RADIATE OUT

TO YOUR WORLD

Full Cover Image

by Solveig Larsen

Crystal Falls

National Park

Australia

Made in the USA
Las Vegas, NV
16 August 2022

53389072R00121